The Mystic Way of
Radiant Love

Alchemy for a New Creation

by

John Francis

Heart Blossom Books, Los Altos, California USA

Published by Heart Blossom Books
P.O. Box 334
Los Altos, California 94023-0334 USA

Cover, interior design, layout and printing by

Ananta Printing & Publishing
Soquel, California.

Printed in the United States of America
10 9 8 7 6 5 4 3 2 1

Library of Congress Catalog Card Number:97-076916

ISBN 1-886063-00-1

Dedicated to the inspiring memory

of

Therese Neumann (1898-1962)
on the one-hundredth anniversary of her birth.
She was truly a forerunner of the New Human.

Table of Contents

Introduction 5

Chapter One
The Anatomy of the Soul 13

Chapter Two
The Mystery of Breath 29

Chapter Three
The Guardians of Paradise .37

Chapter Four
Radiant Love Meditation 49

Chapter Five
Clearing the Way 67

Chapter Six
Trusting God's Radiant Smile 83

Chapter Seven
The New Human 95

Addendum
Mystic Correlations 107

Introduction

Jesus was once asked to state the greatest commandment of God. He replied by quoting a verse in Chapter Six of the Book of Deuteronomy from the Hebrew Bible. "Thou shalt love the Lord thy God with all thy heart, and with all thy soul, and with all thy mind." Jesus then added that there is a second commandment which He said is related to the first. "Thou shalt love thy neighbor as thyself." These two commandments He said encompass all of the Hebrew Laws and the words of the prophets.

Mystics from all the world's authentic religions agree that surrender to the love of God is the way to salvation and "enlightenment." From that immersion in Divine Love naturally flows a compassionate love of one's neighbor as one's self.

The intent of this book is to reveal the mystic way that leads to union with God's Love. This is a path for all and not just a chosen few. We are all called to perfection.

Although mysticism is universal, the scope of this book will be limited primarily to the hidden wisdom found in the Holy Bible. Nonetheless, insights drawn from various mystical traditions will occasionally become apparent throughout the book. The author has written a much larger work of comparative mysticism which someday may be published. You are about to read a highly condensed, extracted version of that manuscript.

True mystics are devoted to feeling God's Love in the here and now. Also, they are concerned with the question:

"Why don't we always feel God's Love?"

To a mystic, God is only far away if we so think. Furthermore, mystics tend to avoid intellectual speculation about what may or may not be the nature of Reality. Hence, they also tend not to be argumentative or authoritarian dictators of belief systems. They have come to the realization that whatever can be known of Ultimate Truth comes from direct and usually "inner" experience and not by mental conceptualization.

It is the conclusion of this author that Jesus taught as a true mystic. Unfortunately, theologians generally seemed to have missed this point for the past two thousand years. Consequently, the mystical parables and sayings of Jesus have either been ignored or given superficial interpretations that miss their original deeper, intent.

When Jesus spoke in parables He said that there would be those who think they hear His words but don't really hear them. In other words, they would be deaf to the inner meaning and not even know it. Saint Paul also warned that the superficial, literal meaning of Scripture is deadly to the spiritual life"the letter kills but the Spirit gives life" (2 Corinthians 3:6).

The deeper meanings of Scripture have been called its soul by the early Church Father Origen. Furthermore, the Jewish mystic Rabbi Simon said that in the future the "inner soul of the soul" of the Bible will be penetrated. Toward this end we have the prayer: "Open my eyes, that I may behold wondrous things out of thy law" (Psalm 119:18).

In this book mystical insights will be offered for a number of parables and sayings which to this date have completely eluded theological "externalism." This word "externalism" is borrowed from the contemplative Father George A. Maloney. Externalists believe that one can achieve union with God by external means alone. It seems surprising but when interpreting the parables of Jesus, most theologians seem to assume that Jesus had an externalist view of life. They apparently have forgotten that He said "the kingdom of God is within you" (Luke 17:21).

The psychologist and Episcopal priest, John A. Sanford, has also commented upon the extroverted state of contemporary theology. In "The Kingdom Within" he states that almost all modern Bible translations say the kingdom is "among" us instead of "within" us—as was the preferred translation of the early Church Fathers.

Today, many theologians are apparently more comfortable with the "kingdom" as a sociological phenomenon found best through interpersonal relationships rather than as an interior, mystical reality revealed through deep meditation. It is no wonder that they have "missed the mark" when it comes to interpreting the mystical parables of Jesus.

Thus after decades of research, I feel confident that this book in your hands offers mystical insights into key Biblical parables and sayings that have long been forgotten by theologians. What emerges is the systematic way Jesus taught His closest disciples to enter into communion with God through silent meditation.

In recent years there has been a resurgence in the practice of mystical, Christian meditation. However, it has been generally justified and explained by pointing to a particular saint who excelled in mysticism and not to Jesus Himself. Also, in many instances Christians, and Jews as well, have looked outside their own traditions because they failed to recognize the mystical gems of wisdom contained within the Holy Bible.

Very little mystical guidance has been drawn from the parables of Jesus or the Hebrew Bible. Furthermore, rarely has it been suggested that Jesus Himself practiced or taught silent, thought-free meditation or any other inner, contemplative discipline.

Unfortunately, this has left proponents of such meditation vulnerable to the loud criticism of noncontemplatives who glibly accuse them of "navel gazing." It is hoped that by revealing the Biblical basis for inner, contemplative practice they will find theological bedrock upon which to justify the mystic way to Life. The world desperately needs to find a way to the inner source of peace.

The reader is probably thinking that it is rather presumptuous of this author to be claiming that he has decoded the mystical parables of Jesus when theologians have been stymied by them for two millennia. Anticipating this reaction, each step along the way in this book has been carefully justified by referring to those whom most readers will recognize and respect.

Also, there will be those who will object to the notion that any new meanings can ever be found in the Bible. This position, however, is contradictory to the teachings of the Christian Church and I believe Judaism also. It is currently an official Church doctrine that the Holy Spirit can still inspire us with ever deeper understandings of Sacred Scripture.

We will demonstrate in this book that Jesus used ordinary language as metaphors to describe the anatomy and breathing of the soul. Furthermore, the approach will not be dogmatic but rather the reader will be invited to test inwardly through experience the validity of the interpretations put forth. This should be a refreshing change for those who have resisted accepting on faith alone that which they find in the pages of the Bible.

The key to these insights came to this author after a particularly "one-pointed" meditation. The words of Jesus, "the kingdom of God is like a mustard seed," arose from the depths of silence. Shortly thereafter, I was guided to discover, by studying comparative mysticism, that the "mustard seed" is an ancient metaphor for the Center Point of the soul.

Once the realization dawned that the language of some of the the parables was mystical, the other pieces of the puzzle quickly fell into place. When Jesus typically began a parable with the phrase "the kingdom of heaven is like..." he was not giving a literal description of Reality. Rather, He was providing mystical insights into how to actually experience God for one's self.

This experience occurred deep within the soul of the disciple whom Jesus personally guided during meditation. This could not occur amid the noisy, bustling crowds that flocked to see the miracle worker from Galilee. Hence, we read that Jesus always took His disciples aside to reveal the deep meanings of His mystical parables and sayings.

The primary commandment to love God with one's whole heart, mind and soul requires a deep surrender to Divine Will. It is not something that can occur by superficially consenting to a particular set of beliefs or rituals. It requires a radical release at the Center of the soul for which mystics often spend an entire lifetime preparing.

Also, a certain type of foreknowledge can also be very helpful. Hence, Jesus did more than give the commandment to love wholeheartedly but also showed His disciples how to fulfill it inwardly.

The idea that knowledge and understanding can facilitate the wholehearted Love of God may seem heretical to some readers. They believe science and religion should be kept separate. However, let us remember that Saint John of the Cross advocated what he called "the science of Love" and lamented that his well-intentioned brother monks did not know the science of inwardly communioning with God. It is hoped that the reader will remember his words when encountering the scientific portions of this book. A few definitions of key words are now in order before we begin.

"Radiant Love" can better be experienced than defined. However, for now it will suffice to say that the unifying, healing, creative, and transforming force of God that emanates from the Center of the soul is "Radiant Love." It should not be confused with biologically-based, hormonal urges and sentiments which are at best forms of counterfeit "love."

"Sacred alchemy" can be defined as the spiritual science of perfecting life. The process whereby Radiant Love transforms imperfect mortal life into immortal life recreated in the ideal "image and likeness of God."

"Meditation" and "contemplation" are two words that are often confused for each other. In traditional, Western-monastic Christianity to meditate means to think about something deeply. For example, a monk might "meditate" upon a certain verse of Scripture by thinking about it in her or his mind. In that same tradition "contemplation" is a nonthinking state of Divine absorption that may be the end result of a thinking "meditation."

However, in common usage today these two words have interchanged their meanings. "To contemplate" now means to think or plan. Whereas the word "meditation" is now used to refer to a process whereby thinking is transcended.

This contemporary definition of meditation may actually be true to its original meaning. The late Doctor Karlfried Graf Durckheim pointed out that the word "meditation" comes from the Latin word "meditari." He was a prominent psychologist, philosopher, and meditation master who did much to revive authentic Christian meditation in the twentieth century.

Literally "meditari" means "being returned to the center." The root "med" means center and is found in such words as median, Mediterranean, and medicine. The latter suggests that medicine was once concerned with our center.

In this book we will use the current definition of meditation which is "a practice that returns us to our center." It is not a thinking process. Thinking is an activity which seems to continually engage most ordinary minds yet does not, in its normal course, lead them to the Center.

The ancient mystical way which Jesus revived and taught to His disciples will be called "Radiant Love Meditation." It is the key to the sacred alchemy of the soul.

These definitions should be sufficient for now. The context within which they occur will also clarify their meaning.

A few more points should be mentioned before we begin. It is recommended that this book be read from front to back. The sequence of chapters build upon each other for maximum clarity. If one reads the chapters out of sequence, misunderstandings are likely to result. This can have especially undesirable consequences when the actual practice of meditation is involved.

Also, in the course of reading this book one may object to a particular statement and feel that the author has not presented sufficient justification. However, if one continues to read it will be discovered that nearly every possible objection has been anticipated and eventually addressed by the author.

Finally, there will be those who find the mystic way presented here simply too radical for them and hence will try to dismiss it as a total heresy. My reply would be that authentic mysticism is inherently radical and thus mystics are necessarily radical people.

The definition of "radical people" given by the eminent theologian Dr. Denise L. Carmody in "The Future of Prophetic Christianity" is a fitting defense of the mystic way.

Those who are spiritually "radical" are "people who desire to go to the depths of the divine love, whence Jesus drew forth his inmost identity and strength."

Chapter 1

The Anatomy of the Soul

Now that the important Introduction has been carefully read, we are ready to proceed inward.

The mystic way of Radiant Love takes one deep into the Center of the soul to be "rooted and grounded in Love" (Ephesians 3:17). From there, the Grace of God is radiated outward into the world in the service of humanity.

The journey inward is greatly facilitated if we have an understanding of our inner being. This domain is what Saint Paul referred to, in the language of his day, as the "inner man" (Ephesians 3:16). We will use the more neutral word "soul" to describe this inner being which we enter during Radiant Love Meditation.

A Hidden Depth

Some of the more mystical parables of Jesus provide us with insight into this inner realm. They have long been misunderstood by those who assumed their simple language referred to the outer world perceivable by the ordinary senses.

First of all, the parables speak of the hidden depth of the soul. They resonate with Christ's saying that "the kingdom of God is within you" (Luke 17:21).

"The kingdom of heaven is like treasure hid in a field"

(Matthew 13:44). We must go beneath the surface of our field of awareness to discover the soul's buried treasure.

In the very next verse we are told the parable of the man who finds "one pearl of great price" in the kingdom of heaven. One must certainly dive deeply to bring up a pearl from the ocean floor.

Jesus also says that "the kingdom of heaven is like leaven, which a woman took, and hid in three measures of meal..." (Matthew 13:33, Luke 13:20). Here again the hidden nature of the kingdom is depicted.

Finally, the kingdom of heaven is a like a mustard seed which initially is buried within the depths of the earth but grows into a large tree. When the sprouting seed breaks through the surface it connects the hidden inner realms to the visible outer world and provides a resting place for the birds of the air (Matthew 13: 31, Mark 4:31, Luke 13:18).

The Center

Mystics down through the ages have dived deeply into the soul and have made a common discovery. The soul has a Center a sacred point of contact where the human and the Divine meet in sublime communion.

The recent renewal of interest in mysticism has seen many contemporary authors explore the theme of the Center. The following are some of their books—all by Roman Catholic priests: "Return to the Center" (Bede Griffiths), "The Hidden Center" (Zachary Hayes), "Finding Grace at the Center" (Thomas Keating, M. Basil Pennington and Thomas E. Clarke) and "Call to the Center" (M. Basil Pennington).

Furthermore, mystics through the ages have described God as a circle whose center is everywhere and whose circumference is nowhere.

If we think of ordinary human awareness as the circumference of a circle then its center is a point. Bede Griffiths says that Saint Francis de Sales referred to the Center as the "fine point of the soul."

Father Louis Massignon of France called the spiritual Center of the soul "Le point vierge"—the virgin point.

Father Massignon shared his mystical insights through correspondence with the American Trappist Monk Father Thomas Merton. Father Merton in turn wrote of the little "'point' or virgin eye by which we know Him! (Christ)" ("Conjectures of a Guilty Bystander," page 160)

Jesus reveals the existence of this Central Point in His mustard seed parable. He is not concerned about being botanically correct when saying it is the smallest of all seeds. Actually, there are smaller seeds. Rather, by calling it the smallest He tells the listener "with ears to hear" that He is referring to the smallest of all things—the infinitesimally-small Center Point.

Jesus also used the metaphor of the "one pearl of great price" to refer to the Central Point. In His parable the merchant is looking for multiple pearls but finds only one of great value. This singularity is a clue to the pearl's symbolism as the one Center Point. Also, a pearl is concealed and is radiant just like the Center Point of the soul.

This leads us to another metaphor Jesus used to describe the soul's Center. "The light of the body is the eye: if therefore thine eye be single, thy whole body shall be full of light" (Matthew 6:22. Luke 11:34). It is noteworthy that

Jesus did not say the plural "eyes" but used the singular. Also, this is no ordinary eye since it does not function in the usual mode as a perceptual receptor but rather itself is a point source of light.

The Christian mystic Meister Eckhart (1260-1327), whom Pope John Paul II quotes according to Benedictine Monk David Steindl-Rast, gives even more mystery to the inner eye. He wrote: "The eye with which I see God is the very eye with which God sees me." Eckhart also described the Center Point as the "seed of God."

In his book "The Inner Eye of Love," Father William Johnston quotes Saint John of the Cross (The Ascent of Mount Carmel, Stanza 3):

> *"With no other light or guide*
> *Than the one which burns in my heart"*

This great mystic seems to have encountered the radiant eye in the center of his being. In mystical literature the word "heart" refers to the inner core of the soul and not merely to the physiological pump.

Regarding this same Light, Saint Peter wrote: "you do well to take heed, as a light that shines in a dark place, until the day dawn, and the day star rises in your hearts" (II Peter 1:19).

Other saints have also referred this interior star. Saint Therese of Lisieux France (1873-1897) called it "the star of love." Saint Symeon the New Theologian (949-1022) wrote of the inner "star that nourishes and heals" and expands (The Hymns of Divine Love, #18).

Finally, the renowned Rabbi Maimonides (1135-1204)

seems to share the same insight with the above when he refers to the "wondrous central point."

Thus we see that the "mustard seed", the "one pearl", the "single eye," and the "star" in the heart are all metaphors that can be used to represent the Center Point of the soul. Each one reveals a different attribute of this wondrous point.

The Heart Cave

Reaching the Center and experiencing its graces requires great discipline. It demands steadiness of attention and subtle perception. It is like threading the eye of a needle.

Actually, this is the metaphor that Jesus Himself used. He said "It is easier for a camel to go through the eye of a needle, than for a rich man to enter into the kingdom of God" (Matthew 19:24, Mark 10:25, Luke 18:25).

The innermost anatomy of the soul can be compared to a needle's eye because the Center Point is enclosed in what could be called a shell which creates an exceedingly small and deeply interior sacred hollow.

This holy sanctuary is referred to metaphorically by some mystics as a "cave." Sister Kathleen Healy explored this theme in her insightful book "Entering the Cave of the Heart."

Jesus referred to the heart's cave using other imagery as well. After calling His disciples "the light of the world" He said "Neither do men light a candle, and put it under a bushel, but on a candlestick; and it gives light unto all that are in the house" (Matthew 5:14,15). A "bushel" is a basketlike container and if placed over a candle would block its light.

Here Jesus is using the metaphor of a bushel basket to refer to the shell which surrounds the Central Light of the soul. This shell forms the walls of the heart's cave. It is clear that Jesus sees into the radiant hearts of His disciples and is telling each of them to bring forth that light and illuminate their body temple called the soul's "house" (Matthew 5:14,15).

This same parable is also recorded in Luke 11:33 with a few interesting changes. There a candle is also not to be put "in a secret place" nor "under a bushel." The cave of the heart might certainly be considered as a secret place.

Also noteworthy, is that the very next verse in Luke's Gospel is the saying: "the light of the body is the eye." So one verse refers to the hidden cave and the next verse reveals the Light at its center or "eye."

A hidden, secret place is also where Jesus told His disciples to pray. "When you pray enter into thy storeroom, and when you have shut thy door, pray to thy Father which is in secret;" (Matthew 6:6).

The New American Bible translation replaces "storeroom" with "inner room." Of course, one could interpret this as advice to merely pray out of public view. However, given the mystical depth of Christ's other sayings and parables we should at least consider that a double meaning may have been intended.

The cave of the heart may certainly be considered a storeroom where the treasures of God's inner kingdom are found. Also, the phrase "Father which is in secret" seems to be pointing us to the interior of our soul and not only to a room in an earthly house. The door which we are to shut would then represent our physical senses through which the distractions of the world so often intrude.

Pope John Paul II in his book "The Way of Prayer" gives a mystical interpretation of this verse. He says "this shuttingin of oneself" results in the "deepest opening of the human heart."

While thinking about inner and outer rooms, the innermost sanctuary of the Great Temple of Jerusalem comes to mind. It was called the "holy of holies" and only the high priest of the temple was considered pure enough to enter it. Could this sacred space be an architectural representation of the cave of the heart?

The anatomy of the soul is also reminiscent of the life-sized, circular labyrinth on the floor of the great Chartes Cathedral in France. A replica has been constructed in Grace Cathedral in San Francisco. A photograph of the original can be found in the beautiful book "The World of Chartres" by Jean Favier.

He tells us that labyrinths were common in medieval churches and were "a symbol of the Christian way."

The labyrinth was used as a template upon which the devotional pilgrim could trace out a walking meditation. One began the journey at the only entrance which was located at its circumference and then gradually followed the tortuous path to its center.

Unlike a maze, with it's dead ends, one is assured of reaching the center in a labyrinth if one is persistent and remains on the initial path. However, this path can meander first toward and then away from the center before the final goal is reached. As we will see, it is an excellent metaphor for the attention which so often wanders in and out during the practice of meditation. The small open circle at the center of the labyrinth corresponds directly with the cave of the heart.

We explained previously that the parable of the "one pearl of great price" refers to the Center Point of the soul. The pearl metaphor is also relevant to our present discussion since a pearl is hidden within the enclosure of a shell and one must dive deeply to find it.

References to the heart's shell can be found elsewhere in the Bible. In The Book of Hosea (13:8) God says that He "will rend the caul of their heart ..." A caul is a covering. In Deuteronomy 10:16 God gives the command to "Circumcise therefore the foreskin of your heart and be no more stiffnecked." Later in Deuteronomy (30:6) we also read "And the Lord thy God will circumcise thine heart, ..., to love the Lord thy God with all thine heart, with all they soul, that thou may live."

It is the hard shell surrounding the heart that inhibits us from feeling the indwelling presence of God's Radiant Love in the depths of our soul. That is the mystical meaning of the numerous other references to "hardened" hearts that can be found in the Bible.

Saint Paul called the heart's shell a veil. Writing about the people of his day he observed: "... the veil is upon their heart. Nevertheless when it shall turn to the Lord, the veil shall be taken away" (II Corinthians 3:15,16).

More details of this heart covering are found in the parable of the hidden leaven. "The kingdom of heaven is like leaven, which a woman took, and hid by mixing in three measures of flour, till the whole was leavened" (Matthew 13:33, Luke 13:21). It is noteworthy that this verse follows directly the parable of the mustard seed.

The number three attracts our attention immediately. What significance does it have? Also, what does the hiding of leaven in the three measures represent? This is obviously a mystical parable since if it was meant to convey a moral or social teaching it would not be so veiled. Therefore being mystical it must refer to the inner life of the soul and hence be consistent with the other mystical parables of Jesus.

We interpreted above the parables that spoke of the shell the encloses the inner eye of the soul. Now the "three measures of flour" that hide the leaven suggests that this shell has multiple layers. Moving inward toward the Center we pass first through the physical, then the emotional and finally through the mental layer of being before entering the silent cave of the heart.

Multiple, inner layers and their corresponding chambers are commonly reported by mystics. For instance, in the Jewish mystical tradition they are called "Kelipot." The rabbis teach that the inner spark of the soul is trapped in these concentric shells.

Meister Eckhart wrote: "A man has many skins in himself covering the depths of his heart. Why, thirty or forty skins ..., so thick and hard, cover the soul" (quoted on page 162, "The Perennial Philosophy," Aldous Huxley).

Also, the contemporary French Jesuit Father Teilhard de Chardin wrote in "The Divine Milieu" (page 131) of the "incandescence of the inward layers of being." Saint Teresa of Avila (1515-1582) in her spiritual classic "The Interior Castle" wrote of her inward journey through seven interior chambers as she is drawn toward the Center of her soul. Please note that one need not be overly concerned as to whether there are seven, three or some other number of inner layers. A given layer may be experienced as having sublayers according to ones own unique spiritual perceptions.

Modern science may have also discovered a phenomenon related to the shells of the soul. The late psychiatrist and researcher Dr. Wilhelm Reich found what he called psycho-physiological "armor" in his patients. This "armoring" he said occurred as the patient tensed and contracted the body to form a shell to prevent certain feelings from reaching conscious awareness. The result of restricting the flow of life energy he said was physical and psychological disease.

The Breath of Life

So far we have explored the inner structure of the soul. We now turn our attention to what makes the soul alive. In the Book Genesis it is written that the Lord God "breathed into his nostrils the breath of life; and man became a living soul" (Genesis 2:7). God's holy breath is certainly more than ordinary air for the soul is of a finer nature than the body of flesh and the oxygen it needs. For lack of a better word we will use the phrase "life energy" to refer to the vital essence of God's breath of life. When this life energy is totally withdrawn from the body no amount of air can revitalize the de-animated form.

Jesus used several metaphors which are suggestive of this life energy. The leaven that is hidden in three measures of meal expands the bread and causes it to be less dense and more porous. Could this be symbolic of an expansion in the soul's radiance and awareness? Do the shells when infused with the life energy expand and become more transparent to inner light? Furthermore, the squeezing and releasing action of kneading dough is similar to the expansion and contraction associated with human respiration.

Another metaphor suggestive of life energy is "lamp oil." It occurs in the intriguing parable of the five wise and five foolish maidens (Matthew 25:1). At midnight the bridegroom comes when all ten maidens are asleep. Upon being alerted they awaken to greet him. However, only the five wise maidens can go in with the bridegroom to the marriage because only they have oil in their lamps. The door is then shut and the five foolish maidens are kept out.

Some theologians see watchfulness as the main theme of this parable. However, if this is so then why are we told that all ten were asleep when the bridegroom arrives. Clearly there is more to this parable than a lesson about the importance of vigilance.

Let us consider that the number five, which is repeated twice, is a key to interpretation. There are five physical senses — sight, hearing, taste, touch and smell. From the mystical point of view, there is a wise and a foolish way of using these senses. In mysticism, lamp oil is a common metaphor for the life energy that is associated with the sensory organs.

A maiden is feminine and hence receptive like a sensory organ. Hence, a sleeping maiden could represent a sensory organ that is still and inactive. The parable thus presents us with sense organs that have entered an inactive ("sleeping") state through either wise or foolish means. The wise way to still the senses is through self-discipline that conserves the life energy ("lamp oil"). The foolish way to sensory stillness is through exhaustion resulting from overindulgence in sensuality which drains the life energy.

The parable would thus be telling us that to enter into the heart's cave (marriage chamber) sufficient life energy is required to illuminate the way. This interpretation is certainly consistent with contemplative experience. Anyone who has tried to focus attention inwardly in contemplation knows how difficult it is to remain alert and responsive when in a fatigued condition. Furthermore, the door that shuts out the foolish maidens may be representative of an inner shell that contracts shut in exhaustion.

Finally, marriage is in a way a union of opposites. Thus, this parable has the added dimension of instructing us regarding the inner discipline required to transcend ordinary, dualistic awareness and feel the Love beyond pleasure and pain.

The very next verse after the above parable in Matthew begins another parable with a metaphor for life energy. This repeats a pattern we have seen before. Parables are presented consecutively in the Bible which share a common theme and complement each other.

We now find the parable of the man who before going on a journey entrusted differing amounts of money to his servants. The amounts were five talents, two talents, and one talent. We are told each man received what was appropriate for this ability. A talent was a considerable amount of coinage that could be as much as seventy pounds of silver.

When the man returned he found that the servants given five and two talents had each invested the money and doubled its value for the master. However, the man who received only one talent hid his money in the ground fearing he would lose it. Angered by this "wicked and slothful servant" the man took away the one talent and gave it to the man who had accumulated ten talents. He then says: "For every one that has, more shall be given, and he shall have abundance: but from him that has not, shall be taken away even that which he has, and cast you the unprofitable servant into outer darkness: there shall be weeping and gnashing of teeth" (Matthew 25:29,30).

Let us assume for a moment that Jesus was not giving a sermon on "prosperity consciousness" even though today in our world such a topic would be quite popular. Rather, let us consider this parable as another one in the series of Christ's mystical teachings regarding the inner life of the soul.

We begin by interpreting the "talent" as a symbol for the coin of the soul's realm. By this we mean that the treasure of the soul is not silver but life energy. In the inner life of the soul life energy is as important for mystical progress as silver is for success in the outer world.

We know that Master Jesus had a way of transmitting life energy to His disciples for use in their inner spiritual quests. Concerning Jesus it is written: "He breathed on them and they received the Holy Breath" (John 20:22).

Such an infusion of spiritual energy can greatly facilitate inner breakthroughs along the contemplative way. It was for that reason that many wished to be closely associated with Jesus as His disciple. Of course the Love one felt in His presence was sufficient for many others as well.

However, each disciple has a different capacity and openness to receive and as the parable says, each was given according to his "ability." Also, there is a parallel with the outer world of money in that the more life energy one already has the easier it is to accumulate even more.

Hence, one is given the life energy to facilitate inner meditation by which it was expected even more energy would be accumulated. However, if one merely tries to hold onto what is given by the Master out of laziness or fear and does not inwardly cultivate more on one's own then even that which he was given will be eventually lost through the normal dissipations of the world.

It is hoped that the reader can see how this parable complements the previous one regarding the wise and foolish maidens. They are both giving valuable instructions regarding the role and the importance of the vital life energy in the inner way of the spiritual aspirant.

The Inner Tree of Life

In the Book of Genesis we read that by eating of the Tree of Life humans can live forever. We will propose here that this Tree is a metaphor for an inner structure within the soul. This inner tree is "rooted and grounded in Love" (Ephesians 3:17). Its roots extend deeply into the universal ground of being.

This tree of life has its origin in the very Center of the soul. Hence, in Genesis we find it in the center of the Garden of Eden. This is also expressed by Jesus in the parable of the greatest tree in the garden which grows from the tiniest seed.

Immediately before this mustard seed parable, Mark's Gospel records another parable which is certainly related. The kingdom of God is compared to a seed that grows from the ground without human knowledge of how it springs and grows. It is mysterious.

Then Jesus describes the sequence of events; "first the blade, then the ear, after that the full corn in the ear" (Mark 4:28). Let us assume that Jesus is not giving His agrarian audience a lesson in Agriculture 101.

When we allow the Center Point to expand in meditation, God's Grace flows into the soul mysteriously like "living water" and vitalizes the tree of life and it grows so that its branches reach upward to the heavens. This tree then becomes a living "Jacob's Ladder."

The roots and branches of this inner tree can be likened to the subtle nervous system of the soul. It is represented as the seven-candled menorah which is the ancient symbol of Judaism. These seven candles have deep mystical significance which is beyond the scope and intent of this book. They are metaphorically referenced in numerous places throughout the Bible, including the final Book of Revelation.

When the interior tree of life blossoms it can have profound physical as well as soul consequences. There is an apocalypse and a metamorphosis. Physically, there is a transformation which begins with the spine, reaches the brain stem and then the brain itself. Hence, "first the blade, then the ear, after that the full corn in the ear."

We are now ready for the next chapter where the mystery of breath will be explored. It is through the Holy Breath that one can receive the precious gift of life energy that was revealed in the parables above.

Chapter 2

The Mystery of Breath

About thirty years ago this author, as a young graduate student, was part of a medical-research team investigating the human respiratory system. My contribution was to create a computer simulation of how gases in the blood affect breathing.

All of us on the research team limited our attention to the natural laws that govern breathing. However, in retrospect I now realize that we ignored two very important factors. The first is the human will.

The respiratory system is somewhat unique in that it is part of both the autonomic and the voluntary nervous systems. By "autonomic" physiologists mean that it can function automatically with conscious intervention.

Yet respiration can also come under the control of the voluntary nervous system as well. For example, by an act of voluntary will one can hold one's breath. However, strictly materialist scientists would reject the notion that the human will is in any fundamental sense "voluntary" or free from the natural laws that govern matter. A materialist is one who assumes that the only laws and forces that ultimately govern the natural world are physical. Free will according to a materialist scientist is merely an illusion. Thus, from this viewpoint a human act which appears willful is actually initiated by natural, physical laws rather than by a force originating in a human will free to make unpredetermined choices.

Most theologians would however strongly disagree with this assumption of science. The human will according to most religions originates in a nonphysical dimension of being often called the soul. It is for that reason theologians argue that the soul is held accountable for the actions it willfully initiates—even after the death of the physical body through which it acted.

When engaged in medical research thirty years ago I had no reason to doubt the mechanistic assumptions of science. However in subsequent years, through the Grace of God, certain unexpected, mystical experiences were bestowed upon this author which revealed unambiguously that the soul is a reality. This once materialist scientist did not even have to make a leap of faith!

Nonetheless, I can still appreciate how difficult it can be to free one's thinking from the materialist indoctrination that is so pervasive in our culture and educational institutions. Were it not for the gifts of faith and interior graces, rampant materialism would certainly swallow every human soul on earth.

It may be helpful to the reader at this point to try a brief experiment for a few minutes. Please sit in an alert yet relaxed and comfortable position. Close your eyes and simply observe the natural process of your breathing. If your attention should wander just gently return your awareness to the breathing. This should be done only for a few minutes at this time.

When finished you may want to write down what you experienced. Did you experience a letting go of some tension that you were not even aware of until it was released? Did a spontaneous sigh of relief occur? Did you feel the emergence of love from the center of your chest? Could this feeling be described as a warm, peaceful, and comforting sense of well-being?

Many who perform the above experiment will feel some release of tension. Subsequently, they will breathe a little easier. This is an important observation since it demonstrates that one may be constricting one's breath by a subconscious act of will that is only apparent when released. Furthermore, it shows that the human will can subtly constrict breathing without entirely stopping respiration.

The relationship between relaxation and feeling of love will be explored in detail in a future chapter. Since God's Will is the ultimate source of true Love it does suggest that the constrictive human will can inhibit the feeling and action of Divine Love in our soul. The action of the Divine Will in the human breath is the second factor mentioned above that scientists ignore when studying human respiration.

The French-Jesuit, mystic theologian Father Teilhard de Chardin (1881-1955) proposed that Divine Love is the hidden, cosmic force in creation driving the soul toward spiritual evolution. This is the Divine Intention behind the Will of Love. Father de Chardin wrote that Christ, the "principle of universal vitality," is partially projected into the heart of matter to guide and "superanimate" this unfolding spiritual evolution. ("The Phenomenon of Man," page 294).

In the discussion that is to follow we will explore how breath awareness facilitates this Divine Intention for spiritual evolution. It is the process whereby the voluntary, constricting human will is released from the breath allowing the Divine Will of Love to recreate the soul into its intended glory.

We will also reveal "the Way" Jesus taught His disciples to inwardly receive the transforming Grace of the Holy "Spirit."

Let us first examine the relationship between the human soul and the Breath of God.

The Holy Breath of God

The word for breath is "ruach" in Hebrew and in Greek it is "pneuma." The later has given us such air and breath-related words as pneumatic and pneumonia in the English language.

Where these two words appear in the ancient Bible manuscripts modern scholars have usually chosen the word "spirit" as the English language translation. The word "spirit" is also found in "respiration" and the related word "inspire."

However, the Jesuit theologian Father Donald Gelpi objects to the common use of "spirit" and argues that "breath" would be more accurate and revealing. Father Gelpi is a highly respected professor at the Jesuit School of Theology in Berkeley, California. He presents his thoroughly researched arguments in the book "The Divine Mother: A Trinitarian Theology of the Holy Spirit."

He concludes that it would be more accurate to replace the phrase "Holy Spirit" with "Holy Breath." Father Gelpi also argues that the Holy Breath is the maternal aspect of God immanent within creation.

We will therefore accept Father Gelpi's expert advice

and use "breath" as a translation for "ruach" and "pneuma" whenever they occur in quoted passages from the Bible.

The resulting phrase "Holy Breath" may initially sound a bit awkward to some ears. However, let us remember that "Holy Spirit" may have also strained some ears originally when it was adopted in preference to the long-standing traditional use of the phrase "Holy Ghost."

It is hoped that relating to God's immanent presence as Breath will open our hearts in a very deep and intimate way to many interior graces.

In Genesis 2:7 we read that God "breathed into his nostrils the breath of life; and man became a living soul." Thus, human creation began with the infusion of God's Breath.

Furthermore, it is God's Breath which continues to generate human life. Job says that "The Breath of God made me, and the Breath of the Almighty has given me life" (Job 33:4). Also, referring to God he says: "In whose hand is the soul of every living thing, and the breath (ruach) of all mankind" (Job 12:10). "All the while my breath is in me, and the Breath (ruach) of God is in my nostrils" (Job 27:3). "But there is a Breath (ruach) in man: and the inspiration of the Almighty giveth them understanding" (Job 32:8). Note, "to inspire" literally means "to breath into."

Jesus too "breathed" on His disciples and said to them "Receive the Holy Breath" (John 20:22). And Saint Paul tells us that "All Scripture is God-breathed" ("theopneustos" in the original Greek).

Furthermore, Paul writes that "by one Breath (pneuma) are we all baptized into one body, whether we be Jews or Gentiles,..., and have been all made to drink into one Breath (pneuma) (I Corinthians 12:13). Finally, the consequence of union with God is a merging into the one Breath. "He that is joined unto the Lord is one Breath" (I Corinthians 6:17).

The feeling of this universal Oneness is the foundation of world peace.

Receiving the Holy Breath

In addition to the above reference to Jesus infusing His disciples with the Holy Breath, many others can be found throughout the Bible.

The psalmist prays to God: "Create in me a clean heart, O God; and renew a right breath within me" (Psalm 51:10).

God replies: "A new heart also will I give you, and a new breath will I put within you ..." and "shall put my Breath in you and you shall live" (Ezekiel 36:26, 37:14). When used in a spiritual context, the word "heart" refers to the inner core of being.

Besides new life, God's Breath can also transport one out of ordinary states of consciousness. "The hand of the Lord was upon me, and carried me out in the Breath of the Lord ..." (Ezekiel 37:1).

Saint Paul reveals how he experienced God by writing: "Now the Lord is that Breath: and where the Breath of the Lord is, there is liberty" (2 Corinthians 3:17). This theme of freedom echoes the psalmist who wrote: "Restore to me the joy of thy salvation; and uphold me with thy free Breath" (Psalm 51:12).

Furthermore, perhaps experiencing God as breath can help us understand what Jesus meant when He said that someday we would "know that I am in my Father, and you

in me, and I in you" (John 14:20). How can we be in
Christ at the same time that Christ is in us? Think of the
analogy of the air we breathe. It is contained within the
atmosphere around us at the same time that it passes in
and out of our lungs.

Gifts of the Holy Breath

The Holy Breath is God's saving Grace. It is through
the Holy Breath that humanity is recreated and paradise
blossom's once again on Earth. When Christ said "seek
first the kingdom of God ... and all these things shall be
added unto you" (Matthew 6:33), He was referring to the
acquisition of the Holy Breath. For truly when one opens
completely to the Holy Breath one's heart is filled to
overflowing.

Since it is impossible to give an exhaustive description
of all these blessings the following list will necessarily be
incomplete.

The first impression that comes to mind is comfort. This
word sums up the deep, soulful feelings of peace, love and
warm contentment that is experienced in the center of the
chest. Actually, the "Comforter" is one of the names given
to the Holy Breath in the Bible (John 14:26). This blessing
is particularly welcomed by those suffering persecution or
rejection by hostile adversaries.

Saint Paul lists the "fruit of the Breath" as "love, joy,
peace, patience, gentleness, goodness, faith, humility, tem-
perance ..." (Galatians 5:22). He also attributes the following diverse gifts to one and the same Breath: words of wisdom, knowledge, healing, miracles, prophecy and the dis-

cernment of spirits (I Corinthians 12). These different gifts are given for the collective good of all.

Of all the above, Saint Paul holds unconditional love called "agape" (in the Greek) greatest of all. This Divine Love is experienced in our hearts by the infusion of the Holy Breath of God (Romans 5:5). It is no coincidence that in English the word "agape" has another meaning and that is "wide open." One's heart must be wide open to feel God's everpresent Love.

This is why Father George A. Maloney gives us the following beautiful definition in his introduction to "The Breath of the Mystic." "The mystic is the one who consciously lets the Breath of God breathe in him."

To this we would add the words of Jesus. "God is a Breath: and they that worship Him must worship in Breath and in Truth" (John 4:24).

Chapter 3

The Guardians of Paradise

In the first chapter, it was shown how the anatomy of the soul is described in the metaphoric language of the Bible. In the second chapter, the Holy Breath of God was revealed as the means by which the Divine pours transforming Grace into the hearts of humanity.

What remains is to actually describe the practice of Radiant Love Meditation by which the alchemical transformation of body, mind and soul is realized through inner communion with God. The keys to this holy way are encoded within the words of Jesus and the inspired saints and prophets of the Bible.

However, before describing the practice it will be helpful to understand the obstacles that block the infusion of Grace. We will see that once the impurities and resistance of the heart are removed, nothing can stop the transforming light of God's Radiant Love. In the words of Jesus, "the Breath is indeed willing, but the flesh is weak" (Matthew 26:41).

The Gatekeepers

Fear and desire, are the two forces within each human soul that block the entrance to the inner tree of life. Fear constricts God's breath of life and desire distracts our attention away from its saving Grace.

Furthermore, fear breeds desire. The contracting power of fear constricts the flow of Divine Life into our inner heart. The resulting soul hunger and emptiness makes us vulnerable to the world of temptations. It seduces us with promises of quick fixes and we are driven further away from inner communion with God at the Center of our being. It is only there that lasting fulfillment is found.

We will first explore the effects of fear and then examine the distractions of desire.

The Fear Barrier

Before proceeding any further let us immediately address a very debilitating misconception. It is that the "fear of God" belongs in the heart of every righteous person and is somehow helpful in the life of a spiritual aspirant. This is the impression that one may get from the numerous Biblical passages that seem to be extolling the virtues of fearing God.

Experience tells us that when we are fearful we don't feel love. This is because fear contracts the soul. The disciple John expresses it so well (I John 4:16,18):

"God is love; and he that dwells in love dwells in God, and God in him.

There is no fear in love; but perfect love casts out fear: because fear has torment. He that fears is not made perfect in love."

Therefore, how can we fulfill the foremost commandment of Jesus to "love the Lord thy God with all thine heart, and with all thy soul, and with all thy mind" (Deuteronomy 6:5, Matthew 22:37) if we fear God?

The answer is that we cannot love and fear at the same time. We can thank the Bible scholars who translated the Hebrew and Greek texts into English for this apparent contradiction. A better translation would substitute "reverence" or "reverential awe" for the word "fear" when our relationship with God is being described.

Now we will examine how fear obstructs the flow of the Holy Breath in our life. This is a problem that is addressed in numerous verses of the Bible.

Fear constricts and contracts and results in hardness. The type of hardness that one gets by tightening a clenched fist. According to the Bible, the result is a hardening of the heart, mind, face, neck, and even one's self.

There are numerous passages in the Bible that refer to the hardened heart. In spiritual language the heart refers to the inner being or soul and not the physiological organ that pumps blood.

The psalmist says "harden not your heart" (Psalm 95:8). In Zechariah 7:12 a stony heart is the reason given for not hearing the inspired word of God's Breath. Jesus attributes the lack of spiritual perception and understanding to a hardened heart (Mark 8:17). And Saint Paul says not to harden your heart if you wish to hear the voice of Christ (Hebrews 3:15).

One very physical manifestation of the hardened heart is the stiff neck. The Lord describes the people of Moses as "stiffnecked" (Exodus 32:9) and the psalmist says "speak not with a stiff neck" (Psalm 75:5). Saint Stephen, the first Christian martyr, was stoned to death shortly after saying "You stiffnecked and uncircumcised in heart and ears, you do always resist the Holy Breath" (Acts 7:51).

The word "stiffnecked" is more than just a figure of

speech. It is a saying that should be taken more literally than it is. The back of the neck does indeed become very tense when the soul is contracted. Saint Stephen expresses the heart-neck connection when he combined the two in the same phrase above.

The reader may want to feel his or her neck right now. That tension can also become chronic during periods of prolonged stress. In fact, such tension can also become chronically embedded throughout the entire body. Such a person has "hardened himself" against God (Job 9:4). He has a hardened face (Proverbs 21:29) and a hardened mind (Daniel 5:20).

Stephen's phrase, "uncircumcised in heart and ears," is also significant. Stephen probably had the words of Moses in mind: "Circumcise therefore the foreskin of your heart, and be no more stiffnecked" (Deuteronomy 10:16).

In a previous chapter, "The Anatomy of the Soul," we discussed the layers of tension that surround and block the central core of the soul. Being "uncircumcised in heart" means that those layers have not been removed.

It is at the very Center of the soul that the Word of God is received through the infusion of the Holy Breath. If that center is veiled, then the Word is not heard. That is the meaning of Stephen's reference to uncircumcised "heart and ears." The inner tensions in the soul thus "resist the Holy Breath."

Desires of the Heart

The focal point of our attention in Radiant Love Meditation is the "one pearl of great price" located deep at the Center of our being. Imagine a precious pearl sitting on the sandy floor of a deep ocean. We are on the surface look-ing down at it. As we dive down to reach it we are like a buoyant cork that is continually being pushed back up to the surface and away from the prized treasure. That buoyant force represents our desires for the surface things of life.

Also, when desires are frustrated or interact with fear all sorts of impure thoughts and emotions are created. Anger, lust, hatred, greed, envy, and worry are just a few of these impurities. We will leave it to the reader to ponder how they come about.

They are impure because they prevent our perception of God. That is why Jesus said "Blessed are the pure in heart: for they shall see God" (Matthew 5:8). The above analogy of diving for the pearl can also be applied here. Our per-ception of the pearl is impaired when agitation creates sur-face waves and stirs up the sandy ocean floor.

It is true that Radiant Love Meditation itself can help to calm the storms of the soul and purify our hearts. However, it is also helpful to avoid those behaviors and mental stim-uli that reinforce fears, desires, and the other hindrances to the inner quest for God.

Actually, a spiritual master may refrain from imparting certain advanced, subtle teachings to an aspirant if he or she is deemed to be too impure in heart to appreciate them or use them wisely. The following story will illustrate this point.

Entering the Needle's Eye

"As Jesus went forth on His way, a ruler came running and kneeled before Him and asked 'Good Master, what shall I do that I may inherit eternal life?'

And Jesus said to him, 'Why call me good? there is none good but one, God: but if thou want to enter into life, keep the commandments.

He said unto Him,'Which?'

Jesus said, 'Thou know the commandments, Do not commit adultery, Do not kill, Do not steal, Do not bear false witness, Defraud not, Honor thy father and mother and thou shall love thy neighbor as thyself.'

And the ruler answered and said unto Him, 'Master, all these have I observed from my youth. What do I still lack?'

Then Jesus, beholding him, loved him, and said unto him, 'If thou will be perfect, go thy way, sell whatsoever you have, and give to the poor, and thou shall have treasure in heaven: and come, follow Me.'

But when the young man heard that saying, he went away sorrowful: for he had great possessions.

And Jesus looked around and said to His disciples,

"How difficult it is for they that have riches to enter into the kingdom of God!

And the disciples were astonished at His words. But Jesus answered again, and said to them, 'Amen, I say to you, Children, how hard it is for them that trust in riches to enter into the kingdom of God!

It is easier for a camel to go through the eye of a needle, than for a rich man to enter into the kingdom of God' " (Matthew 19:16-30, Mark 10:17-31, Luke 18:18-30).

When His disciples heard this, they were exceedingly amazed, saying, 'Who then can be saved?'"

This story is intriguing in many ways. It provides valuable insights into the spiritual life. It also raises many questions.

What really is this young, wealthy ruler asking of Jesus? His initial question is about "inheriting eternal life." If this refers to life after death or even to the final resurrection of the dead, why does he not already feel assured of his "inheritance."

It was a common belief of the day that a rich man, especially one who kept all the commandments of God, would certainly be rewarded in the kingdom of heaven. His good fortune on earth was considered a sign that God was already well pleased with his righteous life. That is why the disciples were "exceedingly amazed" at Jesus' reply.

It is also interesting that while the rich man speaks of "inheriting" eternal life (as a rightful heir inherits property), Jesus speaks of "entering" life and "entering" the kingdom of God. For Jesus "entering" is what the discussion is about.

The "treasure in heaven" that Jesus promises the young man is incidental to actually entering the kingdom of God. That "treasure' which the young man would accrue from giving away his possessions to the poor represents the future blessings he will receive for doing a good, charitable deed. As Saint Paul wrote "whatsoever a man sows, that shall he also reap" (Galatians 6:7). The greater reward however would be for the man to enter the kingdom of God itself. What that means will be discussed in the following.

So we return to our original question. What is this young, rich ruler really asking?

Perhaps he has heard Jesus speak on a number of occasions before. If so, his confidence in his eternal reward may have been shaken by listening to this rabbi's radical parables and sayings.

One thing we can be reasonably certain of is that this young man is no ordinary ruler. Why would the typical man of his social standing be mingling with a heretical rabbi and His band of social outcasts.

Furthermore, the ruler shows great respect for Jesus. He humbles himself by kneeling before Jesus and respects Him enough to publicly ask for spiritual advice.

In turn, "Jesus beholding him loved him." This may refer to the compassion that Jesus showed toward someone who was reaching out to Him for something more than his wealth and station in life provided.

Perhaps, the key to the ruler's mindset is his question asked of Jesus, "What do I still lack?" He may have sensed the peace, joy, and love that radiated from Jesus and his closest followers and felt that despite all he possessed he was still lacking something.

Jesus no doubt understood this man's mind more than this man did himself. What the ruler actually sought was to feel the eternal life of God's kingdom in the here and now on earth. He wanted to enter into the inner circle of Christ's disciples and become "perfect."

The Greek word translated as "perfect" in this story is "teleios." It means mature and in this context it means spiritually mature.

Saint Paul uses this word in ways that are revealing. He writes: "However, we speak wisdom among them that are teleios (perfect): yet not the wisdom of this world, nor the princes of this world, that come to naught: But we speak of the wisdom of God in a mystery, even the hidden wisdom, which God ordained before the world for our glory" (I Corinthians 2:6). Here Paul is saying that the hidden wisdom of God is reserved for the "teleios" — those who are spiritually mature. He reiterates this teaching when he says: "But solid food belongs to them that are teleios (spiritually mature, of full age, perfect) ..." (Hebrews 5:14). "Solid food" refers to deep mystical teachings as opposed to the "milk" of moral precepts which is given to the spiritually immature "babe" who has not yet cultivated the discernment of good and evil.

So perhaps the rich ruler who is "young" in age is also spiritually immature even though he has kept all the moral commandments regarding outward behavior throughout his life.

Nonetheless, Jesus who "loved him" gave this young ruler the opportunity to make the leap to spiritual maturity and join his inner circle of followers. As one of them he would be given the "hidden wisdom" of Christ's parables by direct, inner experience.

However, there was just one condition. This man had to overcome what he "still lacked" and that was an inner trust of God. Even though this man obeyed all the outward commandments of God concerning interpersonal relationships, he was still one of those who "trust in riches." He trusted in riches to bring him security, happiness, prestige, and a counterfeit love from others.

To be an inner follower of Christ he would have to trust totally the Divine Will. He would have to free himself from all external entanglements and attachments.

Jesus put it this way: "No servant can serve two masters: he will hate the one, and love the other; or else he will hold to the one, and despise the other. Ye cannot serve God and mammon (riches)" (Luke 16:13). Similarly, Saint

James wrote "purify your hearts, ye double-minded" (James 4:8).

The problem was not that this man had wealth but rather that he trusted it instead of God. As long as that dependency existed, his mind would always be pulled outward toward his possessions. He could never sit in silent contemplation and receive the inner Graces of Christ in the depths of his soul. This was the intimate way Christ communicated with those who were closest to Him. It still is today.

So when Jesus evokes the implausible imagery of a camel trying to pass through a needle's eye, His words have been carefully chosen to refer to a very subtle aspect of meditation.

The inner process of entering the Center Point of the soul is like threading the eye of a needle. Jesus also referred to this as "entering the kingdom of God." It requires steadiness of attention and acute perception.

As revealed in our previous discussion of soul anatomy, the Center Point of the soul is surrounded by a small shell forming what mystics call the "cave of the heart." This cavity is what the "eye of the needle" represents. The point of contact between the soul and God resides in its Center. It requires great trust and faith in God to narrow one's attention down to that infinitesimally small point and surrender to the Divine Will and Love that radiate from it. Thus, if one trusts more in persons and things than God, those outward attachments will distract and pull the mind away from the Center of Grace.

Finally, it should be made clear that "entering the kingdom of God" does not necessarily mean dying physically and going to heaven. Rather, when we enter God at the

Center of our soul, God enters us. As Saint James put it, "Draw near to God, and He will draw near to you" (James 4:8). In that coming together Divine alchemy occurs. Our body, mind and soul are transformed and heaven manifests on earth.

Buying the Field of Treasure

There is a parable that Jesus told which is worth discussing now because it complements the above story of the rich ruler. "The kingdom of heaven is like treasure hidden in a field; that which when a man found, he hid, and for joy went and sold all that he had and bought that field" (Matthew 13:44).

In the first chapter we discussed that this parable refers to the hidden spiritual treasure buried deep within each soul. One might ask "why did the man have to go out and buy the field if it represents his own soul which supposedly already belonged to him?"

Perhaps the message here is that in a certain sense we do not really have possession of our own soul. A long time ago we sold it to the highest bidder. The payment could have been a prestigious position, a codependent relationship, or some debilitating addiction.

In order to permanently own our soul's treasure we must sell everything (relinquish our attachments) to raise the money to buy back our field of consciousness — body, mind and soul. Only then can we dive deeply in meditation and take possession of the "one pearl of great price."

Actually. the very next verse in Matthew's Gospel is about a man who found "one pearl of great price" and how he sold all that he had in order to buy it. The pearl we revealed is a metaphor for the Center Point of the soul.

Isn't it interesting how the parables and sayings of Jesus are often strung together consecutively like pearls of wisdom to reiterate and expand upon a given subtle theme. Thus, we see that the rich ruler and the finders of the buried treasure and the pearl all had to let go of everything that would prevent them from claiming the inner prize that would truly make them wealthy.

Now that we are aware of the obstacles to be overcome, those who are ready can proceed with the practice of Radiant Love Meditation.

Like the rich ruler, the choice is ours. For that young man more suffering and disappointment was necessary to dis-illusion him with his world. However, there is another way—one of conscious, intentional unfoldment. The reader is invited to "come and see."

Chapter 4

Radiant Love Meditation

The reader will now be entrusted with the "keys to the kingdom." These are techniques and insights which Jesus imparted to His closest disciples. They come to us through His mysterious parables and sayings.

This way of inner communion with God and alchemical transformation will be called "Radiant Love Meditation." Before they were known as Christians, the followers of Jesus were simply called the people of "The Way." In this chapter we will reveal the mystic Way.

The keys of The Way were also known and practiced by the ancient Hebrew mystics and prophets. However, by the time of Jesus the legalistic rabbis of the Great Temple in Jerusalem were no longer practicing the inner Way encoded in their Hebrew Bible.

That is why Jesus proclaimed: "Woe unto you, lawyers! for ye have taken away the key of knowledge: ye entered not in yourselves, and them that were entering in ye hindered" (Luke 11:52). Jesus was speaking about the key to entering into the inner, experiential knowledge of God.

Before that key is given here we should first preview the other side of the door which it will unlock. Radiant Love Meditation is the opening of body, mind, and soul to the endless bounty of God's Grace. Through divine alchemy, this infusion of Grace ultimately transforms the human into an image of God.

Alchemy means transformation and of course there can be no transformation without change. Initially, Radiant Love Meditation brings peace, life energy and a resulting benefit to physical health. Therefore, if one has a chronic disease one should be monitored periodically by a physician for any changes in its status. For example, if one is taking medication for high blood pressure a doctor may recommend a reduction in dosage as meditation naturally heals your circulatory system.

While Radiant Love Meditation is natural and gentle, caution should be observed when there is a severe mental disorder. For example, if one is experiencing deep depression a clinical professional should be consulted before proceeding. Also, in cases of psychosis advice should be sought. These situations warrant caution and close monitoring since meditation does involve the interiorization of awareness.

As one progresses in this contemplative discipline, the guidance of a knowledgeable spiritual director or teacher is also highly recommended. Ideally this person would be a "doctor of the soul." The pathway toward the Center of being has many twists and turns. Therefore, it is helpful to have the guidance of one who has advanced along "The Way." Hopefully, this book will assist in the education of spiritual directors regarding the deeper levels of mystical theology.

Now that the above guidelines have been established the practice of Radiant Love Meditation can be revealed. A fable I remember from my childhood will help set the stage. Little did I realize as a child the deep mystical teaching it conveyed.

The Princess and the Pearl

Once upon a time there was a king. He was very sad because many years before when his daughter was just an infant she was kidnapped from the palace. He had not seen or heard from her since.

So before he died he decided to search his kingdom one more time for his long-lost daughter. He sent out messengers throughout the kingdom and instructed them each to bring all the young ladies of his daughter's age one by one to a palace banquet.

Of course since his daughter was only an infant when he saw her last, there was no way he could recognize her now. So he devised a clever test. When it came for each guest to retire for the evening she was escorted to a specially prepared bedroom.

In the room there was a bed with seven thick mattresses stacked one on top of the other. Each was exceedingly soft and comfortable. The bed was so high it was necessary to climb up a ladder just to reach the top mattress. Upon this bed each of the guests spent the evening sleeping alone.

When morning came and the young woman would come down to breakfast she was always asked the same question by the king.

"How did you sleep my beloved child?"

Invariably the response would be the same. "Oh your highness what a wonderful bed you provided for me. I have never had such a good night's sleep in all my life."

Upon hearing this reply the king was deeply disappointed and saddened. He then had the young woman escorted back to her home and awaited with anticipation the arrival of the next guest. He always hoped that someday he would be reunited with his lost daughter.

Many young ladies came and went. Each one giving the same disappointing answer to the king's special question. Then after three and a half years the day he had been waiting for finally arrived.

When morning came he asked his usual question.

"How did you sleep my beloved child?"

"Oh your highness, I greatly appreciate your hospitality so I hope I do not offend you. To be honest with you sir, I have never slept on such a hard and uncomfortable bed in all my life. I kept tossing and turning all night long. It felt as if there was a large boulder under my mattress.

Upon hearing this answer the king was ecstatic. Alas, he shouted with tears running down his face, "I have found my long-lost daughter! Welcome home my beloved child."

"Your highness, how do you know I am your daughter?" she replied.

"Of the hundreds of young ladies who slept upon those seven mattresses, only you could feel the tiny pearl I buried beneath the bottom of them all. Therefore my dear, you certainly must have the royal blood of a princess to be sensitive to something so subtle."

The Philosopher's Stone

The key to the medieval alchemist's magic was the creation of the Philosopher's Stone in his fiery furnace. Supposedly when a base metal such as lead was touched by this Stone it would be transformed into precious gold.

In the sacred alchemy of Radiant Love Meditation there

too is a "Philosopher's Stone." However, this spiritual stone is not created but uncovered and allowed to work its sacred magic. It already exists at the very Center of our soul. This holy gem can transfigure the mortal human into the immortal image and likeness of the Divine.

Actually, some of the medieval alchemists were depicted searching deep in caves for the prized Philosopher's Stone. Often a fire-breathing dragon was depicted nearby. Such themes are consistent with our descent into the cave of the heart in search of the "one pearl of great price." That cave is the "Holy Grail" sought by all true mystics.

The Center Point is ultimately the primary object of focus in all authentic meditation. It is the point of contact between the human and the Divine. As previously mentioned, it is referred to as the "mustard seed," the "one pearl of great price," a "treasure buried in a field," the "candle under a bushel basket," the "star in the heart," and the "single eye." While each of these metaphors refers to the same sacred point, they each reveal a different aspect of its mystery.

Before moving on, the word "philosopher" itself deserves our attention. It comes from the Greek language and literally means "a lover of Sophia." In the original Greek text of the Bible, "Sophia" is the personification of God's Divine Wisdom. In English-language translations of the Bible, "Sophia" appears as "Wisdom." The ancients knew that true Wisdom comes only through a Love of God.

The Radiant White Pebble

Another metaphor which we have not yet discussed occurs in the highly mystical Book of Revelation (2:17).

"To him that overcometh will I give to eat of the hidden manna, and will give him a white pebble, and in the pebble a new name written, which no man knows but he that receives it."

The Greek word here translated correctly as pebble is "psephos." Unfortunately, some translations say "stone" or "amulet." Both of these lose the important characteristic of smallness which the original word "psephos" (pebble) is meant to convey.

The Flemish, Christian mystic Blessed John of Ruysbroeck (1293-1381) has written a deeply insightful work about this one verse in Revelation. The title "Blessed" indicates he is being considered for official recognition as a canonized saint.

My attention was called to his mystical writings by Roger Corless' book "The Art of Christian Alchemy." I am told that Professor Corless is a member of a Benedictine Order.

The title of Ruysbroeck's work is rendered in English as "The Sparkling Stone" by twentieth century translators. However, it is apparent from his own words that Blessed John is writing of something much smaller than an ordinary stone. He says: "This stone is called a pebble for it is so small that it does not hurt when we tread on it" (all translations by C.A. Wynschenk Dom, "John of Ruysbroeck", London: Watkins, 1951).

John gives us other mystical insights into the nature of the tiny Pebble. We say mystical because they are arrived at through direct, inner experience rather than by mere intellectual conjecture.

He writes that the Pebble is "shining white and red like a flame of fire." This reminds me of the vision of another mystic, Blessed Sister Faustina (1905-1938) of Poland. Some believe her canonization to sainthood may not be far away. Sister Faustina reported seeing Jesus with separate, distinct rays of red and pale (white) light streaming forth from a point in His Sacred Heart. Artists have portrayed this vision and is known as the image of "Divine Mercy."

This similarity with John's description is especially significant since he equates Christ with that tiny Pebble and calls Him "a shining forth of the Eternal Light, and an irradiation of the glory of God."

Finally, for John the mystical Pebble is small, round and smooth and is "a flawless mirror in which all things live." It may seem incomprehensible that the entire creation could be reflected within a single pebble. However, many astrophysicists hypothesize that the whole universe was initially contained within a single, infinitesimally-small point before expanding outward in the so-called Big Bang.

Then we have the very mysterious words of Saint Paul: "But we all, when without a veil see mirrored the glory of the Lord, are transfigured into the same image from glory to glory by the Breath of the Lord" (2 Corinthians 3:18). Is Paul writing about the alchemical transformation that occurs when we lovingly gaze directly into the Central Point, and seeing there the reflected glory of God, are transfigured into that image by the Holy Breath?

If our above interpretation of Saint Paul is correct then he has given us a perfect definition of the spiritual practice we call "Radiant Love Meditation."

The elegance of Paul's "definition" will become apparent as we continue our discussion of the meditation. However, before doing so, we will offer another definition.

Radiant Love Meditation is the sacred alchemical process whereby the innate seed of God, at the Center of the human soul, sprouts and grows into the inner tree of life. The spiritual fruit of this tree transfigures all that is natural into the image and likeness of God.

Another simpler definition is that Radiant Love Meditation is the surrendering of the human breath to the Holy Breath of God.

The Basics of Radiant Love Meditation

The way of Radiant Love Meditation is to surrender to the expansive, transforming Radiant Love of God's Divine Will streaming outward from the Center Point of the soul.

Some preparatory basics will now be given.

Choose a location which is as much as possible free from distractions and potential interruptions. It should be clean, orderly, well ventilated and at a comfortable temperature. Ideally. it is a place used only for your spiritual practice. However, many of us do not have the luxury of setting aside such a space. Of course, if you find yourself away from home you will have to improvise on the location.

At home you may find it inspiring to have an altar in your meditation area with devotional pictures of holy persons for whom you feel love and trust. Incense, fragrance, chanting, and verbal prayers may also be helpful to create a conducive atmosphere. Of course, these are all subject to individual preference. Furthermore, they should not become ends in themselves and distractions from the inner way to Life.

Clean, comfortable clothing should be worn which maintain the body at a normal temperature.

The best time of the day for meditation will vary from person to person. Practice in the quiet, stillness of early morning is a good time to prepare for the coming day. Also a relaxing meditation before retiring in the evening will facilitate a deep and restful sleep. Meditation during the day is helpful in preventing the accumulation stress. It can also clear one's mind to receive needed guidance and inspiration.

Before meals is preferable to after eating. There may be a tendency to fall asleep after a meal. Also, deep states of mediation may interfere with the digestive system. However, this author has found the relaxation of light states of meditation conducive to digestion.

The duration of meditation is determined on an individual basis. One's circumstances will be a major factor. Also, from experience you will learn to sense when a given meditation sitting is no longer fruitful and should be ended.

Assume an alert yet a relaxed posture. Lying down on one's back is permissible if one does not feel drowsy. However, sitting upright with the spine vertical is usually recommended to avoid falling asleep. It may be helpful to feel as if an invisible string is pulling upward on the spine and stretching it slightly. One can be seated in a chair or on the floor in a variety of positions. If seated on a chair the feet should usually be placed firmly on the floor. Sometimes sitting on the edge of the chair is suggested to facilitate alertness. The hands should be placed in a comfortable position.

Keeping the eyes closed will help to shut out visual distractions.

The Alignment of Intention

Perhaps the most often overlooked aspect of meditation is intention. When choosing a particular form of meditation to practice it is highly advisable to determine the ultimate intention of that particular practice. Is the intention congruent with you religious or philosophical convictions? If the answer is no, then something will have to change. If you can't get a satisfactory answer, then our advice is to just walk away from it and don't look back.

The intention should be clearly stated. Clearer intentions give more powerful results.

We will be direct and honest with the reader. In Radiant Love Meditation we align our intention with God's Intention to radiate Divine Love and Light from the Center Point outward to all creation. In that process our body, mind, and soul are alchemically transformed from mortal imperfection to immortal perfection in the "image and likeness of God." More will be spoken of this in the final chapter of this book.

Before actually beginning the practice you may want to silently say a prayer or make an affirmation which states your intention. This would also be the appropriate time to invoke protection and guidance or to affirm your spiritual integrity.

To give you an idea of what an affirmation of intention might sound like the following is a suggestion:

"Let God's Divine Love radiate outward from the Center Point to all of creation. Let this body, mind and soul and all life on earth be healed and transformed into immortal, Divine Perfection." The deeper and more silent this intention is expressed, the more powerful will its effect be. This statement should be addressed to your own inner being. It is not for God's benefit.

Of course, if this all sounds too lofty for the novice then the intention of a little peace of mind and heartfelt love is a good place to begin. In either case, feel free to express your intention in your own words.

Finally, the Divine Intention can be facilitated by a subtle smile which begins on the face and permeates one's entire being all the way into the Center Point. More will be said of the power of the inner smile in the next chapter.

The practice of Radiant Love Meditation itself can be summarized by the following very simple description.

Simply feel breathing.

The reader may now want to put down this book, assume the recommended posture, and for a few minutes inwardly feel breathing.

The Alchemy of Observation

You may be surprised by the effects of such a simple practice as the observation of breathing. Are you now feeling more relaxed, calm, alert, and clear? Do you feel more centered in your body than before? Perhaps you even experienced heartfelt love.

Let us now explore how simply being observant can have such an alchemical effect. During the above experiment you may have noticed times when you felt an effortless release of tension. This was tension you probably were unaware of until it was released. A spontaneous sigh of relief may even have been felt as the tension disappeared and your heart opened.

Saint Paul writes of himself and his congregation who "have the first fruits of the Breath" and "sigh within ourselves" waiting for the "redemption of our body" (Romans 8:23).

"But if we hope for what we see not, we do with patience wait for it. Likewise, the Breath also helps our weaknesses for we know not what we should pray for: but the Breath itself makes intercessions for us with sighs too deep for words." (Romans 8:26).

We are also told that just before Jesus healed a deaf and mute man He looked "up to heaven, He sighed, and said to him, Ephphatha, that is, Be opened" (Mark 8:34).

What is particularly relevant to our present discussion is that the word translated as "sigh" derives from the Greek word "stenos" which means narrow. It is used in the saying of Jesus to "Enter ye at the narrow (stenos) gate ... because narrow (stenos) is the gate, and crowded is the way, which leads to life, and few there be that find it" (Matthew 7:13).

The "narrow gate" refers to the same opening as does the "eye of the needle" (Matthew 19:24) and that is the "cave of the heart" which we have previously discussed.

This is the exceedingly small, hollow space surrounding the Center Point of the soul.

"Ephphatha" could also be interpreted as a command to open the way to this innermost cave of the heart.

This is all interrelated since during the inner observation of breathing there are spontaneous sighs of relief and the effortless narrowing of attention down to the heart's cave and into the Center Point itself.

However, the question still remains: how does just observing breathing result in such deep, inner relaxation?

The key is the subtle shift that occurs from willful engagement in breathing to being a detached observer of the natural, automatic process.

To illustrate the point (pun intended), the reader may wish to try the following experiment. Hold out your hand and make a very tight fist. What is in the center of the fist? The answer is — a tiny, hollow space. That represents the "cave of the heart" at the Center of the soul. The clenched fist itself corresponds to how we chronically hold our breath.

Some of you may disagree and say: how can I be holding my breath if I am still breathing? The holding we are referring to does not completely stop physical respiration. However, it can make the breathing shallow and reduce the total volume of air breathed.

Many readers probably observed the release of subtle, constricting tension during the previous breath-observation experiment and the subsequent expansion of physical respiratory capacity.

What this reveals is that subconsciously we are continually holding on to our breath and thus live in a chronic state of constriction. It is an example of the human free will interfering with a physiological system which was meant to function involuntarily except for rare instances where it is really necessary to hold one's breath to survive an emergency situation.

When we simply sit and feel the breathing process we withdraw from the role of a willful doer and instead become a detached observer. In effect we surrender respiration totally to God-created natural laws. More importantly, by withdrawing our human will from respiration we allow the Divine Will of the Holy Breath to intervene. This Divine intervention results in the alchemical transformation of body, mind, and soul into the immortal image and likeness of God.

This simple act of surrendering respiration to the Divine Will is an act of supreme trust in God's Love. It seems easy enough, especially when one realizes that breathing can function perfectly without human, willful intervention.

However, respiration is not just physical but occurs also on the emotional, mental, and soul levels. So the subconscious holding of breath occurs on those levels as well. This grasping is thus tied into our sense of who we think we are as separate and distinct beings in the world. Holding our subtle breath thus becomes a way of maintaining a sense of separate, autonomous identity apart from the rest of the world. To release our tight grip on breathing is thus interpreted subconsciously as death itself.

The effects of holding onto breath are even greater on the inner levels of being than they are on the surface physical. The heart, mind, and soul can be closed so tightly that only a small trickle of Love and life energy animate them. At the same time there could be more than enough vitality in the physical body for one to lead a vigorous yet superficial life.

As previously discussed the Bible refers to such people as "hard-hearted" and we might say closed-minded as well. In extreme cases, they appear soulless and terrorize the world as tyrannical monsters. They have a soul but it is highly contracted and resistant to Divine Love.

Thus, Radiant Love Meditation comes down to trusting our most basic life process to the Divine Will and allowing sacred alchemy to transform the mortal into the immortal. Jesus spoke of this when He said: "For whosoever will save his life shall lose it: and whosoever will lose his life for my sake shall find it" (Matthew 16:25, Mark 8:35). By grasping at life we die but by surrendering to Life we live immortally.

The Eye of the Storm

In addition to releasing layers of constricting tension, Radiant Love Meditation has another consequence. With repeated practice, our point of view gradually shifts from the surface senses to the "Inner Eye of Love" at the Center of the soul. This phrase also happens to be the title of an insightful book by the Jesuit, Father William Johnston.

This effortless shift to the Center occurs anytime one becomes an observer. The more one is a detached observer, the closer one's point of view is pulled into the Center. The reason is that the only point from which total awareness is possible is the absolute Center of the soul. It is in the same sense that the only vantage point from which an entire landscape can be seen is the very pinnacle of a mountain.

For this centering to occur it is very important that one not react to or indulge in any physical sensations, emotions or thoughts that arise during the process — to do so would be self-defeating.

The closer and more often we move inwardly toward the Center Point the sooner will the day come when we can live in the world permanently established in the eye of love.

The highly respected Cardinal Nicholas of Cusa (1401-1464) writes concerning this over five hundred years ago. God is to be found he says "by entering each day more deeply within yourself and forsaking everything that lies outside ..." "You will rejoice to have found God beyond all your interiority as the source of the good, from which everything that you have flows out to you" ("Nicholas of Cusa," Paulist Press, p. 231).

We feel that outflowing of the good as "Radiant Love."

Just as the stillness in the eye of a hurricane makes it the safest place to be, so too does the Center Point become our haven of peace in a chaotic world. For that reason it is also called the Still Point. This Point is the resting place between exhalation and inhalation. It is the center of the turning wheel that never moves. It is the only place where we can "be in the world but not of it."

The Center Point is also the location from which God's Radiant Love streams outward to transfigure body, mind, and soul. As we move toward it in awareness, surrounding shells of constriction are released and God's Radiant Love expands outward. We then know God's Will from the inside out as the Psalmist writes: "I will run the way of they commandments, when thou shalt enlarge my heart" and "I shall observe it with my whole heart" (Psalm 119:32, 34).

Practicing the Presence of Love

There may be many times when one cannot stop outward activity in the world and sit in silent meditation. Nevertheless, one can always practice an inner awareness of Radiant Love. Be alert for instances when that Love breaks through the clouds of our soul and can be powerfully felt streaming from the heart.

If one is graced during the day by the feeling of Radiant Love, it is an opportunity for remembrance. Should circumstances permit, one would be advised to quickly seize the moment, sit in meditation and become immersed in the Grace of God. Such openings can be fleeting and few and far between.

Finally, let us remember that the smile, both inner and outer, can be practiced in all circumstances. It is one of the best ways to create an inner opening for Radiant Love.

Chapter 5

Clearing the Way

"Make straight the way of the Lord"

Since the Center Point is the "Philosopher's Stone" of sacred alchemy and the "narrow gate" of Radiant Love it deserves our further attention.

Simply observing the breath itself will move our awareness toward the Center. However, there are additional approaches which can facilitate the observation process. They are not necessary and you should not feel obliged to incorporate them into your meditation but they may be very helpful.

To begin with, it is important to understand that breathing involves more than just the physical body. Therefore, while observing the breath one should be alert to the subtle dimensions of breathing that extend deep down into the emotional, mental, and soul levels.

Furthermore, at its deepest levels breathing ceases to be inhalation and exhalation but instead is purely radiant from the Center Point outward. This is expressed Biblically: "The breath of man is the light of the Lord, searching all his innermost chamber" (Proverbs 20:27). God's Light is experienced as Radiant Love emanating from the Center Point of the innermost heart cave. When one begins to feel that Radiant Love, an advanced phase of meditation has been entered. Now we will offer additional insights to help one reach that stage.

Breathing from the Center

When observing a particular level of being, one automatically becomes centered in the next level beneath it. This is because a distance is established between the object and the observer. For example, feeling the physical breath moves one as an observer into the underlying realm of subtle life energy that vitalizes the body. Thus, the more sensitive and observant one is to the full depth of breathing the closer one becomes established to the absolute Center of the soul.

If one is conscientious with regular meditation, each new day's practice will begin a little closer to the Center. Hence, the beneficial effects of meditation are cumulative.

One may want to begin each session by first mentally scanning the entire body for areas of excessive tension. Don't try to relax those areas but just be aware of their presence. Then begin observing the total body breathing as one complete, holistic unit.

From this holistic perspective many find it helpful to next narrow attention to a particular point on the surface the body. Then from that point the breath is felt at increasingly deeper levels as one moves toward the absolute Center Point of perfect stillness.

Energetically speaking, the surface of the body is like a sphere in relation to the interior Center Point. From any position on the surface of a sphere one can move inward along a radius to its center. One can also think in two dimensions and the analogy of all the spokes on a wheel connecting to the same central point in its hub.

However, in the case of the human body moving inward from different possible starting points on its surface will have different consequences. The reason is that different parts of the body will be subject to attention as the focus progresses from the surface to the Center.

For example, yoga teaches that focusing in the head tends to raise blood pressure and focusing on a point below the level of the heart tends to lower it.

Furthermore, focusing on a particular region instead of moving through it toward the interior Center may excite the organs in question. For example, I noticed years ago, when I first began meditating, my attention would get stuck on the physical abdomen and as a result agitate my stomach.

Thus, it is very important in Radiant Love Meditation to not attend to any physical sensations that surface during the meditation. Merely, be detached and let them float by like so many clouds. This goes for emotions and thoughts as well. Be patient with these uninvited guests and they will leave on their own accord if you show no interest in them.

Ultimately, it is only the feeling of God's Radiant Love emanating from the Center Point which will embrace all levels of our awareness. We become detached from everything else in our mortal being.

Those who teach observation meditations similar to Radiant Love Meditation generally specify one of two bodily regions as the starting point for attention—the center of the forehead or the solar plexus region.

This author does not generally recommend beginning meditation by focusing on the forehead, neither do many prominent meditation masters currently teaching today. One well-known teacher has even said there is the possibility of getting stuck in the head region if one is not meditating in the direct physical presence and supervision of a master.

There is another reason for not beginning with the forehead or brain. It seems that most people these days, especially in highly intellectual societies, are already too head-oriented and thus have a lot of energy trapped on the surface of the head. Putting attention there in meditation might only exaggerate an already off-centered awareness.

Interestingly, I have also noticed in such headstrong intellectuals a similar excess of energy at the other end of the spine. Perhaps the phrase "burning a candle at both ends" refers to this syndrome.

This polarized, hourglass-energy distribution is caused by contracting the center. It is like squeezing a tube of toothpaste in the middle and forcing the contents out both ends. Energetically this leaves the central region relatively cold and inert.

This general area of the body, between the two extremes of the spine, corresponds on the physical level with what mystics and the Bible refer to as the spiritual "heart." Thus, one deficient in that area may be cold-hearted and at the same time hot-headed.

Thus, for the reasons stated above it is recommended that the general area of the solar plexus be chosen by those who wish a physical reference point from which to begin observing the breath. This will have the effect of drawing excess energy away from the two extremes into the central region for transmutation.

It should be emphasized that this is just a beginning point of observation. As one's awareness deepens so will one's interior "location."

Also one should be in a feeling rather than a visualization mode. Feelings are of the heart and visualization tends to be head-oriented. It is important to be alert to subtle feelings because this is essential for entrance into the deeper phases of Radiant Love Meditation.

It is the awareness of Radiant Love streaming outward from the Center Point that begins the deeper phase. Furthermore, Love can only be fully experienced through feeling and not by visualization or intellectual analysis.

With surrender to this Radiant Love you will be drawn out of the solar plexus region and up into the inner, spiritual heart region from which this Love radiates. This spiritual heart is centrally located and should not be confused with the physical heart.

Dr. Karlfried Graf Durckheim wrote about this movement upward from the abdominal region to the spiritual heart ("The Call For The Master," Arkana Penguin Books, p.140).

Once absorbed in this Radiant Love, one no longer has any need for meditation techniques found in a book or from any other external source. All the necessary guidance then comes from within.

In these innermost regions the path is too subtle for any instructions that could be put into words. Furthermore, a spontaneity of response is required which cannot be calculated in advance. The great Spanish mystic, Saint John of the Cross (1542-1591), apparently reached this level in his interior meditation. He wrote in "The Ascent of Mount Carmel, Stanza 3:

> "With no other light or guide,
> Than the one which burns in my heart."

Some readers may have found the above references to bodily locations inappropriate in a discussion of meditation. They should be reminded that both Judaism and Christianity are definitely incarnational religions. Therefore, body-inclusive meditation is quite appropriate when the goal is manifesting the Divine Will in the human body.

Furthermore, the correlation of bodily points with spiritual realities has its precedence. For instance, when Christians make the sign of the cross they touch the forehead and say "Father," the solar plexus (or slightly higher) and say "Son," and cross the chest pointing to each lung and say "Holy Spirit" (Breath).

Jesus, the Son, said "no one goes to the Father except through Me" (John 14:6). Perhaps our above discussion of Radiant Love Meditation provides the reader with some insights into the deep, mystical significance of these words of Christ.

Including the body and breath in meditation has long been an accepted practice within the tradition of Christian mysticism. Nonetheless, it seems that it has always been criticized by anticontemplatives—even to this day.

One authentic, mystical tradition which dates back to the early centuries of the Church is called hesychasm. This name derives from the Greek word "hesychia" which means quiet or stillness. The discussion of hesychasm in

"Mystical Theology" by the Jesuit Father William Johnston is highly recommended to the interested reader.

The hesychasts incorporated body, breath, and the Jesus Prayer in their meditation. In the fourteenth century the monk Barlaam of Calabria (1290-1350) visited the Mount Athos monastery in Greece to be initiated into the practices of hesychasm.

He was scandalized by what he observed and appealed in vain to the patriarch in Constantinople to have them condemned as heretics. Barlaam described the experiential, psycho-physiological methods of the holy monks of Mount Athos as "monstrosities" and based on "absurd doctrines." He said they taught of the "differences between red and white lights," nostril breathing, "shields around the navel," and "the vision of Our Lord with the soul that is produced within the navel." (Barlaam's letter can be found in "St. Gregory Palamas and Orthodox Spirituality" by John Meyendorff).

The red and white lights are reminiscent of the previously discussed mystical visions of Blesseds John of Ruysbroeck and Sister Faustina. One also wonders if the "shields around the navel" refer to the shells which surround the Center Point of the soul.

In response to Barlaam's attacks the highly revered Saint Gregory Palamas (1296-1359) wrote his famous defense of hesychasm. It can be found in the appendix to "Early Fathers From the Philokalia" published by Faber and Faber Limited.

Saint Gregory was an archbishop and miracle worker. What he wrote could be taken as a justification of not only hesychasm but of all the breath-related instructions we present in this book concerning Radiant Love Meditation.

He quotes Isaiah 26:18 regarding "the breath of salvation" and refers to the heart as "the secret chamber of the mind." Saint Gregory also writes: "It is not out of place to teach even beginners to keep attention in themselves and to accustom themselves to introduce the mind within through breathing." He also said it is right to use "certain methods to lead the mind into itself."

Saint Gregory describes the deep rest that comes during the observation of breath as "keeping spiritual Sabbath." He also astutely observed that the slowing of respiration is the natural consequence of deep meditation. There is much more that he and the other hesychasts have written that reveals the high degree of sophistication they had reached in the art and science of meditation.

Finally, it is interesting to note that Barlaam accused the holy monks of Mount Athos of "navel gazing." It seems that he was the one who invented this derogatory expression that is still used today by those who ignorantly slander anyone who uses breath as a bridge to communion with God.

If the reader seeks further justification for the place of breath in meditation the following two books are recommended.

"The Beyond Within: Initiation into Christian Meditation" is by Alphonse and Rachel Goettmann. Father Goettmann is a priest in the Orthodox Church of France.

"The Breath of Life: A Simple Way to Pray" is by Ron DelBene with Mary and Herb Montgomery. Father DelBene is an Episcopal priest.

The Prayer of the Heart

Hopefully, at this point in our discussion, it has become

apparent to the reader that Radiant Love Meditation is part of a long, inspired mystical tradition. Over the centuries it has been integrated into the prayer life of many lovers of God—both obscure and well-known. As a result, various prayer methods have been incorporated into the basic practice of Radiant Love Meditation which we described above.

One such practice which the reader may find helpful is called the "Prayer of the Heart" or simply the Heart Prayer. Thoughts and emotions can often be obstacles which block the way into the cave of the heart. However, Heart Prayer uses thought and emotion to open the inner path to the Center.

In recent years, Heart Prayer has become widely known in the West through the publication of a collection of writings called the "Philokalia." They contain the sayings and instructions of the mystical saints of Eastern Christianity. These Christian monks lived in Greece, Turkey, Egypt and in other regions of Arabia.

Their writings span a thousand years and date back to the third century. They have long been a source of deep, mystical wisdom and inspiration throughout the Eastern Orthodox Church. In the Philokalia one can find insightful descriptions of a way of entering into heart communion with God by observing the breath.

Father Thomas Merton, a monk of the Western Benedictine tradition, did much to familiarize English readers with this treasure trove of authentic Christian mysticism.

Heart Prayer incorporates the interior repetition of inspiring words into the rhythm of breathing. In the Eastern Orthodox tradition a brief petition to Jesus is synchronized with the breath and has become known as the Jesus Prayer.

The Jesuit priest Father Anthony de Mello gives a helpful discussion of the Jesus Prayer in his very popular book "Sadhana: A Way to God." The late Father de Mello was from India and sadhana is an Indian-Sanskrit word which means spiritual discipline.

He describes how the Christian Orthodox prayer, "Lord Jesus Christ, have mercy on me," can be repeated with the breath.

"Lord Jesus Christ" is silently verbalized on the inhalation and "have mercy on me" is on the exhalation. Father de Mello informs us that in the Eastern Orthodox tradition the word "mercy" is used to mean more than forgiveness of sins but also "grace and loving kindness."

An important point is worth mentioning now. The more subtle the vocalization of sound, the more deeply will the words penetrate into the soul. Speaking out loud is the grossest level of articulation. Subvocalizing a word under one's breath is a deeper level. Finally, just listening inwardly for the sound of an intended word is perhaps the most subtle level of all.

Heart Prayer facilitates Radiant Love Meditation in several ways. First, it prevents mental chatter from distracting one's attention away from the breath. This is because the mind can hold only one verbal thought at any one instant of time. Also, the devotional nature of Heart Prayer enhances receptivity to God's Love and purifies the soul of negative emotions.

Finally, after continued practice Heart Prayer takes on a life of its own and breathing becomes prayer and a constant remembrance of God's presence. It seems that the words themselves become embodied within the breath which prays them without end. Thus we see how Saint Paul's advice to "pray without ceasing" can be fulfilled (I Thessalonians 5:17).

Another verse suggests that Saint Paul experienced what might be called spontaneous, inspired Heart Prayer. "God has sent forth the Breath of his Son into your hearts, crying out, Abba, Father" (Galatians 4:6).

Saint John of the Cross commenting on this verse in his "Spiritual Canticle," (Stanza 38, p. 515, E. Allison Peers, Doubleday Image Book,1961) gives such an interpretation. He writes concerning Galatians 4:6, "the soul that is united and transformed in God breathes in God into God the same divine breath that God, being in her, breathes into her Himself ..." In other words, in the state of inner union there is one Holy Breath that is being exchanged between the soul and God.

This reminds us that Jesus breathed on His disciples and they received the Holy Breath (John 20:22). The Breath of Jesus crying out "Abba" from our hearts may actually be a reference to the sound heard in deep states of soul breathing. If one listens attentively, "Ab" can be heard on the inhalation and "ba" on the exhalation. It might also refer to the sound made by a deep, spontaneous sigh of surrender to the Holy Breath.

The Breath of Christ may also be mentioned in another verse. Jesus said "Take my yoke upon you, ..., and you shall find rest for your souls. For my yoke is easy, and my burden light" (Matthew 11:29, 30).

Surrendering to the Holy Breath of God during Radiant Love Meditation could be compared to being harnessed to a yoke that is "easy" and "light." Furthermore, the "rest" that is found for the soul could refer to the "peace that passes all understanding" (Saint Paul, Philippians 4:7) that is felt when breathing momentarily stops or "rests" during deep states of relaxation and surrender.

Since we have been discussing sounds associated with Heart Prayer, a closing observation is in order. Father de Mello reminds us that there are many possible sounds that can be repeated with the breath.

For example, the late Father John Main in his book "Word Into Silence" states that his "mantra" is the Aramaic word "Maranatha" (Ma-ra-na-tha) which means "Come Lord." Father Main cofounded with Father Laurence Freeman the "World Community for Christian Meditation"—a contemplative "monastery without walls."

In Father de Mello's homeland, India, mantras have traditionally been repeated along with the breath. Actually, they are felt and heard by experiencing breathing in deep states of meditation. It is reported that the sound "Ma" is felt on the inhalation and "Om" on the exhalation of the breath.

These two sounds are considered very sacred. "Om" is chanted during the liturgy of Roman Catholic Masses in India. It is experienced as the primal sound of God's creative Word and revered in the same way as the Hebrew word "Amen." The word "Ma" is said to open one's heart to the maternal Grace and Love of God. Children throughout the world cry out "Ma" when they want their mother. It is thus interesting that the Aramaic word "maranatha," which means "come Lord" begins with the sound "ma." Also, the Hebrew word "hochma," which is used throughout the Hebrew Bible for the personification of God's maternal wisdom, also ends in "ma."

Finally, the reader may be wondering how different sounds can be heard within the breath. A scientific analysis of complex sounds reveals that they are composed of a spectrum of various different frequencies. Perhaps, by listening at different depths and locations one tunes in to particular frequencies and thus perceives different sounds. This is just a hypothesis put forth for the inquiring mind.

The Power of Scripture

In a previous chapter we discussed at length how fear and desire are the two great obstacles that guard the entrance to the Center of Grace. It was recommended that when they give rise to thoughts and emotion one should simply let them pass without reacting. However, there may be times when they are particularly persistent and therefore it is advisable to adopt another tactic.

Certain verses from the Bible can be recalled which counteract the fear or desire. Of course, one must already have them in memory since the practice of meditation would be interrupted by opening a Bible to read a verse.

Before recalling a counteracting verse it is helpful to recognize the origin and nature of the specific emotion or thought and whether it is fear-based or desire driven.

We will now offer a few verses which may be helpful. By searching Scripture yourself many more will be found.

If one is distracted by persistent thoughts concerning bodily needs one might recall some of the words of Jesus recorded in the Gospel according to Matthew, Chapter 6. It contains a number of verses that might be very helpful during meditation.

For example, "Take no thought for your life, what ye shall eat, or what ye shall drink;" (Matthew 6:25).

"Life is more than food, and the body is more than raiment" (Matthew 6:25).

"Which of you with taking thought can add one cubit to his stature?" (Luke 12:25).

Suppose desires come as a general restlessness that says there are more important things you should be doing instead of meditation. You might recall these words of Jesus: "Seek ye first the kingdom of God;... and all these things shall be added unto you" (Matthew 6:33).

Also if you feel pulled in two opposing directions during meditation try recalling the verse : "No one can serve two masters" (Matthew 6:24).

Fear may also emerge during meditation for a number of reasons. If so, one may recall the words of Saint John the Apostle "God is love" and "perfect love casts out fear" (I John 4:18).

Fear may also cause a crisis of faith during meditation. Christ's words "be not of doubtful mind" (Luke 12:31) may encourage you.

Furthermore, you may experience fear as your awareness and sense of self is focused down to the infinitesimally-small size of the Center Point. The following saying of Christ may have been intended specifically for this crisis of faith: "If ye have faith as a mustard seed, ... nothing shall be impossible for you" (Matthew 17:21).

Also encouraging as one "shrinks down" to the size of the Center Point are Christ's words: "he that humbles himself shall be exalted" (Luke 18:14).

If the mind is particularly agitated and obsessively

churning thoughts, one could turn to it and simply recall the words of God: "Be still!" (Psalm 46:10).

In response to thoughts and feelings of resentment or retaliation one may recall the words of Jesus on the cross: "forgive them; for they know not what they do" (Luke 23:34).

Also, if one is feeling anger over some injustice or evil the words "it is better to light a candle than curse the darkness" could be helpful.

Finally, there comes a time during deep states of meditation to abandon all techniques and practices and simply surrender to God's Love which radiates outward from the Center Point. As Saint John of the Cross put it "when the end is reached, the means cease" ("Spiritual Canticle," Stanza 37, p. 515).

These beautiful words of Jesus may come to mind: "Consider the lilies of the field, how they grow; they toil not, neither do they spin;" (Matthew 6:28). Will not God clothe you in a garment of Radiant Love equally as beautiful?

If we assume that Jesus was not advocating laziness or passivity then perhaps the above saying is not referring to the outer world of work. Rather, He may have actually been indicating the proper attitude of surrender necessary for deep states of inner communion with God.

We will conclude with a few key points regarding the use of Scripture verses during inner communion. First, the more subtle and silent the remembrance of the verse, the deeper will it penetrate. It may seem paradoxical but ideally the words should be recalled at a level too deep for words.

One way to facilitate this is by bringing to conscious awareness only the first few words of a particular verse.

For instance, just subvocalize "consider the lilies ..." and let the rest of the verse be recalled by itself at a deep, subconscious level.

The following observation may be related to the above. When Hebrews and Christians in Biblical times wanted to quote from Scripture they often would only recite the first few words of a passage because the listeners usually knew the rest of it anyway. Another reason may have been that allowing the listener to internally recall the unspoken words was more effective than hearing the word outwardly pronounced by the speaker.

In the next chapter our discussion will shift to nonverbal means of facilitating meditation.

Chapter 6

Trusting God's Radiant Smile

"Peace begins with a smile."

Mother Teresa of Calcutta

The reader may have noticed that the word "concentration" has not been used in this book. This is because many have been conditioned to believe that to concentrate one's attention on something requires tensing and grasping onto the object of interest. Actually, just the opposite results from detached observation—profound relaxation and deep surrender.

In our basic discussion of Radiant Love Meditation, effortless observation was presented as a necessary and sufficient practice. However, one may encounter highly resistant tensions that block the flow of God's Grace. Therefore, we will now offer some techniques the author has learned from yoga which have proven helpful in such situations. Hopefully, they will not become ends in themselves and substitutes for surrender to God's Grace.

One may even feel that these techniques run counter to our intention to enter a state of effortless surrender. However, consider a golf club that has been permanently bent out of shape—a sad sight. To straighten the club it is necessary to bend it in the opposite direction.

The Inner Smile of God

The human smile is recognized worldwide as a sign of goodwill. Should it therefore be surprising that the Jesuit and mystic, philosopher Father Teilhard de Chardin reveals in the "Divine Milieu" his perception of the universal Smile of God present in all of creation.

There's a saying: "Smile and the whole world smiles with you. Frown and you frown alone." This is because when we smile it is a way of aligning our will with God's Will and we thus experience the universal Smile. However, we do have the option of frowning in contradiction to God.

Mother Teresa of Calcutta said: "Peace begins with a smile."

Another saint from India, the Holy Mother of Kerala, has said: "...learn to smile always with your whole heart. Try not to let the smile fade from your face."

The wisdom of these two saints is very profound. When we smile it relieves tension in the face and head. Physiologists have even discovered beneficial biochemical changes induced by the simple act of smiling.

What is not generally known is that the whole body as well as the face has the capacity to smile. If we define smiling as radiating the soul's inherent goodness then a smile is not limited to just the face.

The reader can only appreciate the mystical smile from inner experience. A simple exercise will now be offered.

Please assume your normal posture for Radiant Love Meditation with eyes closed. Let a gentle smile come upon your face. Now with your awareness scan the rest of your body. Is there an area that feels particularly tense? If so please project the sense of smiling from your face to the region. Then, feel as if smile is emanating from that area. Is there a release of contracting tension? You may now want to subtly smile with your whole body, mind, and soul. Do you feel the radiation outward of love, peace and joy?

Inner smiling is a subtle practice. It can be used to release the various layers of concentric tension all the way down to the Center Point of the soul. That's what is meant by smiling with the "whole heart." Remember, the more subtle the smile the deeper its effect.

Tensions in the abdominal region can have a particularly constricting effect on the flow of life energy throughout the body. One of the effects is tightness on the surface of the head. Inner smiling along the spine from its base up to the level of the solar plexus can often miraculously dissipate stubborn constrictions.

This holistic smile can also become the way in which we continually relate to others and life in general. It makes negative thoughts and emotions almost impossible. One may even want to force the face into a smile to counter the body's stressful reactions to the trials of the day. The beauty of inner smiling is that it can be done in all circumstances.

Despite its many benefits the mind may resist smiling. It may say "why should I smile if I am not feeling happy." The answer is that happiness will follow a smile. Furthermore, one does not need a reason to smile nor permission from the mind.

A negative, mental reaction to smiling may be the result of living in an environment surrounded by people who rarely smile. It seems that on a subtle level the facial expressions of others can impress themselves upon our inner being thereby leaving a lasting effect—either positive or negative upon the inner flow of our life energy. An internalized frown may be a source of resistance to the practice of inner smiling.

Whoever first said "smile, be happy" was definitely expressing deep wisdom.

Finally, some readers may conclude from the above discussion that smiling is no laughing matter. Actually, one could think of laughing as convulsive smiling. Deep belly laughing is a wonderful way to dissipate abdominal tension and why we love a good joke or a funny story. Perhaps, that's also why successful comedians laugh all the way to the bank.

Inner Exercises

Exerting exercise to relax tensions in body, mind or soul can be counterproductive. Sometimes if one just becomes aware of a tense muscle it will automatically relax. This is the value of mentally scanning the body before beginning a meditation session.

Another effective strategy is to consciously tense and then release those areas that are under chronic tension. This gets one in touch with those areas and the extra tension seems to at least temporarily exhaust the persistent contraction.

A second technique involving muscle contraction will now be presented. However, this author has hesitated quite a bit before deciding to put it in print. The only reason it is given is because it has proven so beneficial to so many people. The author's concern is that the reader may feel it is totally inappropriate in a spiritual book. But come to think of it, this may be the reaction of many readers to much of this book.

The yogis teach that by constricting and relaxing the anal sphincter muscle, which controls the anal orifice, tensions in the musculature of the head can released. I have also personally found that it brings some relief to sinus headaches. Yoga suggests it can be done during one's normal daily routine of activities and has health benefits that prolong longevity.

Now returning to mysticism, if this sphincter muscle is only mentally constricted and released without physically affecting the muscle itself the subtle layers of tension surrounding the Center Point of the soul will often loosen.

Sole Breathing

Another effective technique for draining excess energy away from the head is to bring one's attention down to the bottom of the feet and feel the pulsation of respiration in and out of the soles. Perhaps there is some mystical reason why "sole" and "soul" are pronounced the same. Incidentally, this exercise is recommended while lying in bed for those who have difficulty sleeping at night.

Not Tongue-in-Cheek

Finally, the next procedure is recommended for maintaining an uninterrupted flow of subtle energy throughout the body during the practice of meditation. It is said that placing the tip of the tongue on the roof of the mouth completes a circuit for vital life energy to flow up the spine, around the top of the head and then down the roof of the mouth through the tongue and down the front of the body. One should not let a conscious placement of the tongue be a distraction because if the energy flow is intense enough the tongue will automatically be drawn upwards to complete the circuit anyway.

The energy-steering effect of the tongue reminds me of a Bible quotation from Saint James. "Behold also the ships, which though so great, and driven by fierce winds, are turned about with a very small rudder, ... even so the tongue is a little member, ..." (James 3:4,5).

In closing this section a few comments seem appropriate. First, one should not let the above suggestions complicate one's inner meditative life. Simpler is better. These techniques are offered for situations that may arise.

Secondly, in advance stages of Radiant Love Meditation the inner working of the Holy Breath may become pronounced and many spontaneous occurrences are possible. For example, the fingers may move together to complete energy circuits. Detached surrender is usually recommended and not active resistance if phenomena occur. A knowledgeable spiritual director can be very helpful in such situations.

Trusting Radiant Love

Radiant Love is the Grace of God that can alchemically transfigure the mortal human into an immortal image of God. It streams into the soul as "living water" from the depths of the Center Point. All that we must do to be "born again" is release our death grip on that fountain of Grace.

This is an act of deepest surrender to the Will of God. It requires an extraordinary depth of faith and trust. Hence, many approach the inner gate but "few are they that enter in." The whole intention behind the mystical theology of Radiant Love Meditation is to facilitate that interior opening.

Faith and trust work together in meditation. Saint Paul gives us a helpful definition here. "Now faith (pistis) is confidence in the expected, and the belief in things not perceived" (Hebrews 11:1).

Much of the discussion in this book so far has been to cultivate the reader's faith. It is a faith in the real existence of God's transforming Grace at the Center of the soul. If the reader chooses to practice Radiant Love Meditation regularly, then you will "have faith as a grain of mustard seed" (Matthew 17:20) that grows from something tiny into a great tree of life reaching up to heaven.

Trust, on the other hand, is the act of giving that seed of God an opening to sprout and grow. We must surrender all fears concerning what will happen when we release our constraining grasp upon the Center Point. We simply trust that the loving Creator of that seed has only our highest interests at heart and will guide its fruitful growth from the depths of our soul.

God is Love and trust grows each time we are immersed in the Radiant Love that casts out all fear.

The spiritually mature surrender because they are pulled inward by a thirst for God's Grace. However, the novice too often must suffer the pain of sin over and over again before making the leap of faith. A Sufi mystic had this in mind when he said "Pray for thirst, not water."

Perhaps, herein lies the mystery and meaning of suffering. Does God allow suffering so that we will become disillusioned with superficial-surface living and seek refuge and comfort from the heart's inner cave?

The late Father John Main is considered one of the great Christian meditation masters in the twentieth century. He understood the trust required to narrow one's attention down to the Center Point. To the false self it seems as if life is being extinguished as one's attention is focused down to an infinitesimally-small point. However, once one passes through this "narrow gate" and "needle's eye" which Christ spoke of a remarkable expansion of awareness occurs.

Father Main wrote in "The Inner Christ" and "Word into Silence" that "to come to that one-pointedness we need courage." The reward he said is an "infinite expansion of love."

The importance of trusting the inner presence of God is a recurring theme in the messages communicated to Blessed Sister Faustina by Jesus. Her diary entitled "Divine Mercy in My Soul" records these inner words from the Lord. Jesus told her "I am dwelling in your heart as you see Me in this chalice" (#1820). She was also given the simple prayer "Jesus, I trust in you."

Sister Faustina was told by Jesus that lack of trust constracts the soul. Furthermore, it is only by trust that the graces of God's mercy are drawn and "the more a soul trusts the more it will receive" (#1578).

She was also told to live according to God's Will "in the most secret depths of your soul" (#443). Jesus said it also displeases Him whenever we don't allow the Divine Will to be our will.

Most meaningful to me was the message: "When a soul approaches Me with trust, I fill it with such an abundance of graces that it cannot contain them within itself, but radiates them to other souls" (#1074).

One may ask how can we know God's Will moment-to-moment so that we may obey it? This is the fruit of Radiant Love Meditation. We eventually discover that the Divine Will is continually emanating from the Center Point of our soul and can be felt as Radiant Love.

If our trust is complete this Radiant Love can fulfill every need and aspiration of our life. This Radiance will even inspire the thoughts we need when we need them.

Hence Jesus said "take no thought how or what thing ye shall answer, or what ye shall say: For the Holy Breath shall teach you in the same hour what ye ought to say" (Luke 12:12).

This requires a great deal of trust and subtle, inner attunement to the Center Point. We are speaking here about entrusting one's thinking process to Radiant Love.

One asks "how can I discern between those thoughts that are Divinely inspired and those which are not?" Those which have emanate directly from the Center Point are Divinely inspired. By practicing detached inner observation one learns to detect the direction from which thoughts arise. Those which come from the absolute Center Point are always of Divine Origin for they come from the very "mouth of God."

It is a very delicate, subtle procedure to not think thoughts but instead to allow them to be effortlessly inspired from the Center Point outward. There is a certain subtle, inner attitude and orientation which one learns to adopt. One becomes centered, graceful, and trusting in all circumstances.

Trying by effort to stop thinking is futile and misses the point (pun intended) of being open to Divine inspiration. Thoughts per se are not the problem but the thinking of them by human effort and will is a hinderance to union with God.

Saint Teresa of Avila recognized this nonthinking state as an advanced stage of contemplative prayer. She was wise to say that one should not try to force one's way into it but allow it to unfold as a natural, graceful progression of the interior life. When one becomes inwardly immersed in Radiant Love this state becomes effortless and automatic.

Today, the numerous, vocal anticontemplatives are absolutely terrified by the thought of entering this state of graceful nonthinking. They seem to have adopted the rationalist's motto "I think therefore I am." For them to desist from the incessant churning of mental chatter, for even one moment, is synonymous with death and anihilation.

However, the biggest fear they voice is that by entering into an interior state of nonthinking that they will be in some way inviting the Devil himself to do their thinking for them.

This fear is obviously nothing new since Jesus addressed it two thousand years ago. He said: which of you would give your son a scorpion if he asked for an egg? "If ye, being evil, know how to give good gifts to your children; how much more shall your heavenly Father give the Holy Breath to them that ask Him?" (Luke 11:13).

In other words, if your true intention is to receive the Holy Breath of God in your meditation then God will not send the Devil instead.

It is significant that just before the above saying Jesus had told the parable of the man who opened his door only because of the persistence of the knocker. This Jesus followed by the saying: "seek and ye shall find; knock and it shall be opened."

This inner door is a reference to the entrance to the cave of the heart. The knocking is the required repetition of an inner spiritual discipline that is necessary before the inner door to God's Grace is flung open.

Another concern of the anticontemplatives is that interior, wordless prayer will produce a thoughtless person—one who is preoccupied with selfish desires. Nothing could be further from the truth.

Actually, the fruit of Radiant Love Meditation is thoughtfulness and caring. In the purified heart thoughts are inspired by the Holy Breath of God and not by the false self. Furthermore, caring, kindness, and compassion are the virtues that naturally flow from immersion in the Radiant Love of God.

Divinely inspired thoughts are also original and creative. One might even say they can be "radical" in that they radiate outward along a radius from the Center Point of the soul. Isn't it interesting how the roots of words sometimes contain a deep wisdom generally unrecognized today?

Finally, this author wishes to address those who should know better but nonetheless condemn wordless contemplation as wrong. Their attention is called to the "Way of Prayer" by Pope John Paul II. He states, in this inspiring little book, that sometimes his prayer involves speaking to God and sometimes it involves no words at all. At those wordless times the Pope says he listens all the more intently.

The Pope has evidently learned from his long life of deep, silent prayer that thinking thoughts interferes with hearing that "still, small voice" of God which Elijah the prophet heard (I Kings 19:13).

In conclusion it seems appropriate to note the famous words of Saint Augustine which are quoted by the Pope. "You have made us for yourself, O Lord, and our hearts are restless until they rest in You" (Confessions, I.1).

I rest my case.

Chapter 7

The New Human

"Behold! I make all things new."
The Book of Revelation 21:5

In recent years various techniques for stilling the mind have gained widespread popularity. However, the important role that intention plays in these practices has often been overlooked.

Peace of mind is usually a sufficient result for most meditators. This is understandable since we live in an increasingly hectic and turbulent world. Many seek health and others pursue creativity. Pyschic powers entice others. For some, there is a more specific objective such as improving one's tennis or golf game. Finally, there are those who pursue something called "enlightenment."

If any of the above are the reader's objective, then so be it. Every journey begins from where we are.

However, in all the religions of the world that acknowledge the existence of God there is one ultimate intention for meditation and that is surrender to the Divine Will.

The first step toward this surrender is to align the human intention with the Divine Intention. Therefore, those who choose this path are confronted with the question: what does God intend for humanity?

A nontheist of course is not concerned with such a question. They either explicitly deny the existence of a Supreme Being or believe it is better to pretend as if one does not exist.

This is no place to debate the existence of God. Such intellectual exercises are usually not very fruitful anyway. Rather, it does seem appropriate to simply repeat a wise saying: "Someone who says there is no God is like a person who says 'I have no tongue.'"

Nontheistic meditation traditions, while ignoring God, nonetheless generally do have an intention which goes beyond the mundane desires of most humans. Their intention is simply to escape from the suffering of life. They practice mental disciplines which they expect will lead to annihilation and thus permanent freedom from what they perceive as the suffering inherent in life. This intention may or may not be explicitly stated along with their techniques and rituals.

It is important to be aware of this intention if one is considering a journey all or part of the way along one of these nontheistic paths. Even if one believes their so-called annihilation is impossible, consideration should be given to the hidden effects of a meditation practice which is not consciously aligned with the Divine Intention.

So this brings us back to the question: what is the Divine Intention for humanity? I do not wish to get in trouble with all the religions of the world—one is sufficient. Therefore, I will limit my comments to Christian Biblical prophecy. However, I know of prophets from the other great traditions which share in principle the same general vision that I will now propose.

The Revelation

In the last book of the New Testament we have recorded a revelation of Jesus Christ given to a mysterious person named John who was exiled on the island of Patmos by tyrants of the Roman Empire.

This Book of Revelation is generally considered to be one of the most difficult to understand in the Bible. The language is highly symbolic. This author believes it has remained so enigmatic to theologians because they fail to recognize that much of its language refers to the inner realm of the soul. Instead, they attempt to force an entirely outer-oriented interpretation upon the metaphoric-language of the soul.

This author contends that the Book of Revelation depicts both an inner as well as an outer time of revolutionary change. The inner and the outer are always complementary in the realm of spirituality.

Perhaps, this author will elaborate on the details of the Book of Revelation in a future work. For now, a brief discussion will have to suffice.

We will focus our attention on those referred to as the chosen ones—the 144,000 "of all nations, and kindreds, and people, and tongues" (Revelation 7:9). They emerge at the end of the age (aion).

The Greek word "aion" has been frequently mistranslated as "world." Hence, many think the events prophesied will occur safely in unforeseeable future when the entire "world" will end.

These chosen ones are the first of humanity to undergo the baptism of Divine Fire that completely transforms their mortal bodies into immortal temples of God. There are three baptisms; water, Holy Breath, and Divine Fire. Jesus referred to the later baptism when He said: "I have come to send fire on the earth" (Luke 12:49). This fire alchemically transmutes human "lead" into Divine "gold."

This transformation of the chosen is foreshadowed by the baptism of fire that occurred at the Feast of the Pentecost. Pentecost was an annual Jewish feast to celebrate the first fruits of the year that were harvested from the fields. That small group in the upper room who received the Holy Breath of God anticipate a similar event to occur on a global scale.

The significance of the number 144,000 is that it represents the critical mass of transfigured humans necessary to facilitate a much larger transformation on a planetary scale. Once this first group has been physically immortalized, they in turn create a field of Light which makes the way easier for the rest to have their bodies also transformed.

This effect was revealed by Jesus when He told His disciples "Ye are the Light of the world" (Matthew 5:14). He also called them the "salt of the earth." This later is a reference to how a relatively small mass, "salt," can preserve a larger mass from decay.

The biologist Dr. Rupert Sheldrake in his book "A New Science of Life" has proposed a hypothesis that may have some relevance here. He postulates the existence of an etheric resonance field which acts as a collective memory that records the evolutionary accomplishments of a species. All members of a species can tap into this memory field.

It is worth noting that Dr. Sheldrake was a friend of the

late Father Bede Griffiths. He wrote "A New Science of Life" at Father Bede's Benedictine Monastery in India.

The effect of this resonance-memory field is that an evolutionary breakthrough by one member is accessible to other members of the species that resonant with it. Hence, it becomes easier for another member to replicate the previous advancement.

Of course the 144,000 could also facilitate human spiritual transformation through teaching, healing, and by setting an example as well as being instruments of Divine Grace.

Those who are not physically present on the Earth when "critical mass" is reached need not despair. The prophecy says they will be returned to the physical Earth plane to eventually be transformed themselves.

There is another reason why there should be no anxiety about not being among the first "harvest." We are all immortal already even without the transformation of our bodies. The purpose of having an immortalized-physical body is to serve God more perfectly on Earth. That service involves the transformation of Earth back to a Garden of Paradise.

Before one can have the natural body immortalized it is necessary to overcome the fear of death. Thus. one who experiences the metamorphosis is not trying to escape death but is rather bringing real Life to Earth. It is compassion for the suffering that motives one to undergo the disciple and sacrifices necessary to be one of the 144,000.

The Prophetic Vacuum

It is unfortunate that religion today has not been able to communicate this vision of the Divine Intention for life on Earth. As a result a great spiritual vacuum has been created.

At this time in Earth's history more and more people are beginning to sense that physical death, disease, and suffering are not ultimately inevitable. Their intuition tells them that they have a great inner spiritual potential that can be unfolded in the here. and now.

Unfortunately, many of them have not been able to find support for those aspirations in their own religions. As a result, they have gone off into the marketplace of strange ideas seeking some sense of spiritual fulfillment. Many are so hungry for deep wisdom that they are willing to eat spiritual junk food out of the trash bins of pseudospirituality.

While mainstream religions are reluctant and even embarrassed to preach about the creation of the New Human, many cults have arisen to fill that vacuum. They are preaching suicide, genetic cloning, group orgies, and contact with unknown space aliens as means to achieve the "next level above human." They twist and distort the words of Jesus and some even deny the existence of God. Instead, they say humans were created in a test tube by aliens. Tens of thousands believe them.

Perhaps what is most disturbing is a growing trend to characterize death and destruction as a way to transcend the human condition or usher in a new millennium. It is a healthy development that death is becoming a lessed feared prospect. However, the pendulum may be swinging too far because religion has failed to positively affirm the possibility of heaven on earth in the here and now. What will happen if those with weapons of mass destruction become infected with delusional beliefs of apocalyptic salvation?

This insanity is possible because there is such a lack of spiritual discernment in the public at large. If religion would preach, using scientific, mystical language, the real power of God's Holy Breath to transform humanity many souls would be saved from the deceptions of pseudoscience and twisted theology.

The Divine Intention

Answering our original question, the Divine Intention as stated by Christ and the Hebrew prophets is that we "might have life" and have it "more abundantly" (John 10:10).

Furthermore, "God shall wipe away all tears from their eyes; and there shall be no more death, neither sorrow, nor crying, neither shall there be any more pain: for the former things are passed away" (Revelation 21:4). This is a promise for embodied Life on earth and not some reward in a distant, ethereal heaven.

Father George A. Maloney relates this to meditation which he calls "mystical prayer." He writes in "The Breath of the Mystic" that mystical prayer is not just for inner purification but is also "a resurrection, a rebirth, a re-creating process into the New Man."

So before beginning Radiant Love Meditation we clearly align our intention with that life-giving Divine Intention. You can choose your own words to affirm that alignment. For example, "let God's Radiant Love transfigure this body, mind, and soul into an immortal instrument for the healing and resurrection of all life on Earth."

Throughout this book we have attempted to reveal how the Bible contains the keys to the manifestation of the New

Human through sacred alchemy. Every human soul has the capacity to receive the inner grace of Radiant Love.

When the soul totally trusts the inner Light of Love it no longer is dependent upon externals for survival. Furthermore, this Radiant Love has the intelligence and energy to maintain an embodied-conscious presence on Earth uninterrupted by the phenomenon we call death.

Also, this new human will be ideally suited (no pun intended this time) for travel throughout the infinite cosmos. Since she or he is immortal, and requires no food or air, the vacuum and vast distances of space are no obstacles. Also, fatigue and sleep never occur since there is direct access to the infinite energy of Love through the Central "zero point" of the soul.

Our space program would be wise to focus on human transformation before attempting to venture out into the unknown. Progress will be swifter in the long run if we master inner space before venturing toward outer space. The most advanced civilizations on other planets and dimensions have learned this lesson. The "right stuff" for an astronaut is the Radiant Love of God.

The Saintly Forerunners

We do not have to rely on Biblical prophecy alone for our knowledge of the Divine Intention for the New Human. Down through the centuries there have been numerous saintly persons of all religions who have embodied one or more of the attributes which will someday be common in all of the New Humanity.

Michael Murphy has made an extensive study of these

spiritual prodigies in his awe-inspiring book "The Future of the Body." Mr. Murphy is the co-founder of the Esalen Institute which was instrumental in the ending of the Cold War.

In reviewing his widely-acclaimed book, the Catholic Book Club wrote: "The Future of the Body will broaden the intellectual horizon of anyone interested in what authentic incarnational spirituality ought to mean in our time."

It includes cases of auras, bilocation, levitation, and incorruptibility of holy cadavers. However, I was most impressed by the well-documented accounts of persons who no longer required food to live. Imagine the tremendous freedom which would come from not having to take food or drink in order to maintain the physical form.

One such account was of the mystic, stigmatist Therese Neumann (1898-1962) who is documented to have taken no food or drink for the last thirty years of her life. A revealing encounter between her and Paramhansa Yogananda is recorded in his fascinating book, "Autobiography of a Yogi." She explained her fasting by proclaiming "I live by God's light." Furthermore, Therese disclosed that "One of the reasons I am here on earth today is to prove that man can live by God's invisible light, and not by food only." (Hey kids, don't try this at home without adult supervision!)

A Call for Renewed Vision and Cooperation

There is a saying that goes something like this: "Where there is no vision the people perish." It seems that we as a planet have lost the vision of the possible human. We have also forgotten the ancient promise that someday paradise will return to Earth as it is in heaven.

Instead of aligning our intentions with this Divine Intention, we settle for something much less. The virtual reality of consumerism and immediate gratification has become the new "opiate of the masses." Religion too often is used merely as an aspirin for life's hangovers.

The prophesied heaven on Earth will not fall out of the sky as a reward for well-intentioned ignorance. It is only by applying the "science of love that are hearts are purified and prepared to receive the transforming power of God's Grace.

The great mystic Saint John of the Cross lamented that his fellow monks knew not how to receive God's Grace even though their prayer life was well-intentioned. He coined the word "science of love" to describe the systematic, inner wisdom needed to align the human will with God's Will.

Religions need to dive deeply and rediscover the "science of love." If they don't, religion will be perceived as irrelevant in the new millennium. I shutter to think what will take its place.

There are those within every religious tradition who are laboring to resurrect the science of mystical theology. They need encouragement and support and not ridicule or condemnation. They are the "salt of religion" that preserves its mystical core.

More specifically, mystical prodigies need to be recognized and nurtured. They are the foremost candidates to form the "critical mass" needed to give birth to the New Human. Spiritual directors should be initiated into mystical theology so that they may shepherd those who would "enter through the narrow gate."

Spiritual communities also need to be formed to provide protective and enlightened environments where those who are ready to be "perfect" (teleios) may blossom and be transformed into the New Human.

Finally, authentic religion has a heavenly mandate to intelligently communicate the Divine Intention for heaven on earth to its entire congregation. There should also be an outreach and dialogue with all facets of society concerning the Divine Intention. We can be assured that God's Vision for earth will prevail in a loving environment of humility and openness. This goodwill is inevitable and natural when the feeling of Radiant Love prevails in every heart.

Truth cannot be compartmentalized into separate and competing categories. The Oneness underlying diversity must be allowed to emerge. Only through cooperation, mutual understanding, and respect can global metamorphosis occur.

All members of the planetary body must live in cooperative harmony if our final destiny be not tragedy but transfiguration.

Addendum

Mystic Correlations

Just before this book was typeset for printing, I learned of the life and writings of a most remarkable, saintly woman. Fortunately, an unexpected delay in publication made it possible to insert this addendum before the presses began to roll. Perhaps the delay was caused by Divine Providence intervening to ensure that the reader learned of important, inspired messages that are very relevant to the major themes of this book.

The holy woman was named Luisa Piccarreta. She lived in Corato, Italy from 1865 to 1947. For the last 64 years of her life she neither ate nor drank and rarely slept at all. At the age of 22, Luisa became bedridden for the rest of her life (no pun intended) yet she was always "fresh as an Easter lily" and serene.

It is reported that beginning at the age of nine she inwardly heard the voice of Jesus and later had visions of Him. Throughout Luisa's life she often entered into mystical states, which sometimes lasted many days, where her body became rigid as if dead.

In obedience to her spiritual director, Luisa recorded 36 volumes of messages from Jesus Who described their content as a "most sublime science." The first nineteen have been released to the public and the remainder are still being critically evaluated by Church officials. Those that are available have received the official "Imprimatur" of the

Roman Catholic Church after years of close examination. The "Imprimatur" is given only to works that have been deemed to be free of errors which contradict Church doctrine. It is also noteworthy that as of 1997 the cause for her eventual canonization to sainthood is making favorable progress.

I have only just begun to study Luisa's writings, however, my attention has been caught by the number of correlations between her messages and the findings of my many years of scholarly and mystical exploration. This is particularly significant since Luisa had no more than a first-grade education and apparently had no access to scholarly works of theology. Nonetheless, her messages from Jesus reveal subtleties of mystical theology which are not widely appreciated or even taught in colleges and seminaries.

For instance, Jesus told Luisa about the "Eternal Point" which now only has life in Heaven but will soon flow towards earth to mold its souls and that this Eternal Point is immensely infinite (p128,129 "When the Divine Will Reigns in Souls"). Also, Jesus said that "prayer is a single point" (p94, Book of Heaven, Volume 7).

Furthermore, we are told that the soul comes from the "Divine Center" to which it will return (Volume 7). Jesus also said to Luisa: "Whoever lives in my Volition must be as a center of everything" (p6, Volume 13). He then went on to describe such centered souls as radiant suns.

Of particular relevance to our previous discussions about meditation is what Jesus said to Luisa in Volume 17 about the Divine Breath. He said that it is necessary for His Breath to enter into the human soul to restore the Divine Will there (p13). The Divine Will is called the "air for the soul" (p58). It should "penetrate to the depths of the soul with all Its riches to carry to the soul divine food, life, rapturing virtue from all that is above, invincible strength, the fecundity of all the virtues and every good" (p58).

Jesus concluded His discourse on the Breath with this advice: "I recommend that if you want my Will to accomplish in you Its designs, breathe always the air of my Will so that as you breathe It, the Life of the Divine Will may live in you and conduct you to the true purpose for which you were created."

That purpose is for the Divine Will to be done "on earth as It is in Heaven." Jesus told Louisa that a New Era will soon come upon the earth when the original-paradise conditions of Eden will be restored through the action of the Divine Will.

Correspondence and Mailing List

Correspondence may be addressed to the author in care of Heart Blossom Books. Any comments or suggestions regarding this book would be greatly appreciated.

The author is available for media interviews as well as lectures and seminars. If the reader would like to make suggestions for such appearances please forward the appropriate information.

Finally, if you would just like to have your name placed on the confidential Heart Blossom Books mailing list, we would be pleased to receive your address and any other contact information. We will then be able to notify you of forthcoming books and activities in your area.

Ordering Information

If your local bookstore does not yet stock THE MYS-TIC WAY OF RADIANT LOVE, it can be ordered directly from the publisher:

Heart Blossom Books
P.O. Box 334
Los Altos CA 94023-0334

Price: $8.88 per book.

Sales Tax: California residents please add 8%.

Shipping and Handling:
USA book rate—$2.00 first book, 50¢ for each additional book.
Priority Mail (USA only)—$3.50 per book.

Canada—$3.50 first book, 75¢ for each additional book.

Overseas—please inquire for rates.

Please make checks payable to: Heart Blossom Books.

Prices are subject to change.